PHILOSOPHICAL LETTERS

The Library of Liberal Arts

The Library of Liberal Arts
OSKAR PIEST, FOUNDER

The Library of Liberal Arts

PHILOSOPHICAL LETTERS

VOLTAIRE

Translated, with an Introduction, by
ERNEST DILWORTH

Associate Professor of English, Lehigh University

• •

The Library of Liberal Arts
published by
THE BOBBS-MERRILL COMPANY, INC.
A Subsidiary of Howard W. Sams & Co., Inc.
Publishers • Indianapolis • New York • Kansas City

Francois Marie Arouet de Voltaire: 1694-1778

PHILOSOPHICAL LETTERS was originally published in 1732

· · · · · · · · · · · · · · · · · · ·

CONTENTS
· · · · · · · · · · · · · · · ·

PHILOSOPHICAL LETTERS

INTRODUCTION

There are two things the *Philosophical Letters* can do for twentieth-century people besides amuse them. One is to introduce them (and for this purpose it is as good as any book I know) to the eighteenth century and to those two complementary strains of what, in our deadly provincialism, we call the Western Mind: the French and the English genius. The other is to remind them that there is hope for men because they have it in their power to be reasonable.

Professional philosophy the book is not; it is, however, a collection of critical reports by a *philosophe* of the Age of Reason—that is, a rational observer and free-thinking moralist —interested in the human meaning of all thought and action. The separate letters or chapters are written more or less as if to a friend in France (Nicolas Claude Thieriot), and the book first appeared, in an English translation by John Lockman, as *Letters Concerning the English Nation* (London, 1733). Voltaire himself referred to it often enough as the "English Letters," but it was as *Lettres Philosophiques,* with an additional letter on Pascal, that the book, on June 10, 1734, was condemned by the Parlement of Paris to be lacerated and burnt by the hangman, as "likely to inspire a license of thought most dangerous to religion and civil order." The true work of Voltaire had begun, and our lives are different because of it.

We think of Voltaire as having been, even in his cradle, a wit, a poet, a freely discursive mind. In the story of Ninon de Lenclos' leaving him 2,000 *écus* to buy books with, nothing is more interesting than that when she died, in 1705, he was no more than eleven years old. He was young enough when introduced into the urbane and hedonistic society of the Temple; at twenty-five he was famous as a tragic poet, the author of another *Oedipus.* Ambitious, inquisitive, always busy, he was also a brilliant speculator, and at thirty he had an independent fortune. His genius and individuality were irrepressible, and he was already, as the author of *La Ligue,* known as an epic poet, as well as a critic of powerful institutions and men, when he was called away from dinner with the Duc de Sully and cudgeled in the street by hirelings of the Chevalier de Rohan. After a comfortable stay in the Bastille (it was his second), where he was sent so that he might be protected from his own desire for revenge, he was released on the provision that he keep fifty leagues away from Paris. He went to England.

We do not know the dates of arrival and departure, but we may suppose his visit to have lasted from about the end of May, 1726, to September or October, 1728—that is, roughly two and a half years. Nor do we know much about his life in England, though he seems to have mixed with a fair number of notabilities if only because of the recommendations of Englishmen whom he had known in France—among them Bolingbroke and Horatio Walpole, the British ambassador. We hear of his being with Bubb Dodington, with Lord and Lady Hervey, with Pope, with Gay, and with Mrs. Conduit, the niece of Newton. He met the dowager Duchess of Marlborough; he talked with Berkeley and with Edward Young. It seems that he was, with Swift, for three months the guest of Lord Peterborough. He thought highly enough of Swift to write letters of introduction for him, in June of 1727, to du Noquet, treasurer-general at Calais; to the Comte de Morville, Secretary of State; and to the Marquis de Maisons. The first six months he spent in learning English, partly by means of constant attendance at the theater; by December of 1727 he had written and published two essays in English—one on epic poetry from Homer to Milton, the other on the civil wars in France.

Other travelers had written on the English, particularly during the previous half-century. The book Voltaire finished in 1733 was not so much a description of England and the English as a series of notes on the good life of men and nations. If he had pleased to comment at any length on English eccentricity, for instance, it would have been in the vein of this passage from a letter to Rolland Des Alleurs:

I assure you again that a man of y^r temper would not dislike a country, where one obeys to the laws only and to one's whims. Reason is free here and walks her own way, hippocondriaks especially are well come. No manner of living appears strange; we have men who walk six miles a day for their health, feed upon roots, never taste flesh, wear a coat in winter thinner than y^r ladies do in the hottest days.[1]

Reason is free here and walks her own way. . . .
In the *Philosophical Letters,* Voltaire is on the trail of principles, though no book could seem more casual or be more informally put together. That is one of the principles. These letters are not to sound like art. He is talking, without guile or labor it would seem (though the guile will often step forth and preen itself for the pleasure of author and reader); he is talking to everyone who can pause long enough to listen. To a translator, doubly concerned with language, the vocabulary seems limited, repetitious; in the *Philosophical Letters* there are no great adventures in style: the grace of precision, the delicacy of strength will shine in works to come. This is mere life. And so Voltaire jerks his thumb at the subject with *ce, ce, ce*—this man, this book of this Jones; and so, the translator may now and then feel, the sentences go on, to end in the last murmurs of a subordinate clause. The translator finds that sentences constructed with such unconcern come over into English sounding absurdly ragged; but his infrequent and reluctant shifting of a clause only proves to him the colloquial beauty of the original, the style in style-lessness, the grace of mind when the mind is by nature full of ideas. There is possible triumph in being caught without one's wig.

And the immediate subject matter of these notes? English books and writers Voltaire reports on briefly, for the most

---

[1] Letter No. 391 in *Voltaire's Correspondence,* ed. Theodore Besterman (Geneva, 1953–.)

part; it is important for his countrymen to know that this
home of science and of political and religious liberty has
poems and plays worth reading. He glances at their faults as
well. The faults of literary works are not so mysterious as the
beauties. A Butler makes a great comic poem out of subject
matter near to him in place and time; too much of it is meaningless to foreigners and to Englishmen of a later generation.
A Shakespeare—and Voltaire was to feel, with some justice,
that it was he who had introduced Shakespeare, Newton, and
inoculation to the French—a Shakespeare has marvelous
beauties in him, but barbarism as well. Barbarism is the toler-
ation or enjoyment of disorder, deformity, horror, and the
truly civilized will not admire it as colorful, or excuse it because of poetic beauties elsewhere. Barbarism is indefensible,
and the best that poetry can do is remind us of the fact. This
classical view of things, absorbed by Voltaire from the air of
France, from Boileau, and from the Jesuits who schooled him,
is more rational than some moderns appear to think. It assumes that literature is not cut off from life, that poetry is
necessarily social, that all things are vitally related to one another, that thought and action have consequences, and that
what we admire is much of what we shall come to be.

Voltaire's interest in literature, then, while not unaesthetic,
is broadly humane. He must survey and report on Bacon and
Locke, even Pascal, for the same reason as he must report on
the Parliament. He sees man at the center; he catches at what
may make us free and throw light on the world for man's sake.
Though granting the genius of Pascal, he sees in him a bent
for the antihuman; though he admires the candid manliness
of the Quakers, he scorns their artifices of spirituality; though
he understands that mathematics paces off the immeasurable,
he stares metaphysics in the eye and firmly, on a giddy planet,
stakes out our claim. There is work to do on earth; it can be
done only if enough men are sufficiently aware of their earthly
circumstances. Voltaire is not a democrat but a liberator. He
sits down to the subject of scientific method as to the practical
questions of government. He is one of the great eighteenth-

century popularizers, men who upheld with such passion the value of humanity that they forced the specialists out of their towers, and shamed them into lucid conversation.

For the rest, whether the subject is Quakers or Presbyterians, smallpox or universal gravitation, and whether we are simply enjoying the detail of the moment, we are hearing good news about man: that in his simplicity he is admirable; that he need not be superstitious; that slavery is not inevitable; that science is part of common sense; that reason and instinct are equally gifts of God; that there is no law by which we must make a hell of our earth rather than a garden; above all that we are on our own, helped by no providential hand, and that to be intelligent and just is our responsibility and our finest achievement.

ERNEST DILWORTH

SELECTED BIBLIOGRAPHY

EDITIONS OF VOLTAIRE'S WORKS

Oeuvres complètes de Voltaire. Edited by A. Beuchot. Paris, 1828.

Oeuvres complètes de Voltaire. Edited by L. Moland. Paris, 1877-85.

Lettres Philosophiques. Edited by Gustave Lanson. 2 vols. Paris: Société des Textes Français Modernes, 1909; 3rd ed., 1924.

Lettres Philosophiques. Edited by Henri Labroue. Paris, 1910; 5th ed., 1931.

Lettres Philosophiques. Edited by Raymond Naves. Paris, 1939.

Lettres Philosophiques. Edited by F. A. Taylor. Oxford: Blackwell, 1943; rev. ed., 1946.

COLLATERAL READING

Ballantyne, Archibald. *Voltaire's Visit to England, 1726-1729.* London, 1919.

Besterman, Theodore (ed.). *Voltaire's Correspondence.* Geneva, 1953.

———. *Voltaire's Notebooks.* 2 vols. Geneva, 1952.

Brailsford, H. N. *Voltaire.* London, 1947.

Chase, Cleveland B. *The Young Voltaire.* London, 1926.

Collins, J. Churton. *Voltaire, Montesquieu, and Rousseau in England.* London, 1908.

Havens, George R. "Voltaire's Marginal Comments upon Pope's *Essay on Man*," *Modern Language Notes,* XLIII (1928), 429-439.

Lanson, Gustave. *Voltaire.* Paris, 1919.

Lecky, W. E. H. *A History of England in the Eighteenth Century.* 8 vols. London, 1878-90.

Mornet, Daniel. *French Thought in the Eighteenth Century.* Translated by Lawrence M. Levin. New York, 1929.

Stephen, Leslie. *History of English Thought in the Eighteenth Century.* 2 vols. London, 1902.

Tallentyre, S. G. *The Life of Voltaire.* 2 vols. London, 1904.

Torrey, Norman L. "Bolingbroke and Voltaire," P.M.L.A., XLII (1927), 788-797.

————. "Voltaire's English Notebook," *Modern Philology,* XXVI (1928), 307-325.

OTHER ENGLISH TRANSLATIONS OF THE
Philosophical Letters

Letters Concerning the English Nation, by Mr. de Voltaire (London, 1733). This first translation, by John Lockman, preceded by a year the first edition in French. The letter on Pascal did not appear in this edition or in the French edition published in London in 1734. The Lockman was several times reprinted.

The Works of M. de Voltaire, translated from the French, with notes, historical and critical, by T. Smollett, M.D., T. Francklin, M.A., and others (London, 1761-65, 1761-70, 1778-81). As in France, the letters were now to be found in volumes of Miscellanies.

Letters on England, "Cassell's National Library" (London, 1886). This was the Lockman translation.

The Works of Voltaire; a contemporary version with notes, by Tobias Smollett, revised and modernized new translations by William F. Fleming and an introduction by Oliver H. G. Leigh, a critique and biography by the Rt. Hon. John Morley (Paris, New York, London, Chicago, 1901).

Letters Concerning the English Nation, with an introduction by Charles Whibley (London: Peter Davies, 1926). This was a reprint of the first edition of Lockman's translation. The edition was limited to 750 copies.

NOTE ON THE TEXT

The text used as the basis for this translation is that of Jore (Rouen, 1734), as established by Gustave Lanson in his critical edition of the *Lettres Philosophiques* (Paris, 1909). The translator has also consulted with great profit the editions of Raymond Naves (in the *Classiques Garnier*), Henri Labroue (Paris, 1910) and F. A. Taylor (Oxford: Blackwell, 1958). The footnotes, without exception, are those of the translator and for this reason have not been bracketed.

Because the text which Voltaire used for his references in the letter on the *Pensées* of Pascal is very different from the text which is consulted today, we reprint, for convenience of reference, the table included in Naves' notes to Letter XXV, "On the *Pensées* of M. Pascal."

Pensée I: Brunschvicg, fragment 430.

II: 430	XV: 642	XXVIII: 199
III: 434	XVI: 793	XXIX: 556
IV: 430 and 47	XVII: 578	XXX: 63
V: 233	XVIII: 565	XXXI: 266
VI: 646 [1]	XIX: 585	XXXII: 209
VII: 619	XX: 610	XXXIII: 593
VIII: 620	XXI: 97	XXXIV: 327
IX: 631 and 630	XXII: 172	XXXV: 170
X: 479	XXIII: 139	XXXVI: 378
XI: 477	XXIV: 139	XXXVII: 165
XII: 571	XXV: 139	XXXVIII: 180
XIII: 757	XXVI: 139	XXXIX: 68
XIV: 607	XXVII: 139	XL: 62

[1] I have not been able to verify or correct Brunschvicg references 646 and 200.

VOLTAIRE
[François Marie Arouet]

PHILOSOPHICAL LETTERS

LETTER ONE

ON THE QUAKERS

Since it seemed to me that the doctrine and history of so extraordinary a group as the Quakers deserved the curiosity of a thinking man, I went, in order to instruct myself, to visit one of the most famous Quakers in England, a man who, after thirty years in trade, had been able to set a limit to his fortune and to his desires, and had retired into the country near London. I sought him out in his retreat; it was a house small but well built, unornamented and decent throughout. The Quaker himself [1] was a fresh-looking old man who had never had an illness because he had always been a stranger to the passions and to intemperance. I have never in my life seen anyone with more noble, or more engaging, an air.

He was dressed, like all those of his religion, in a coat without pleats in the side, and without buttons on either pockets or sleeves, and he wore a large hat with the brim turned down like those of our clergy. He received me with his hat on his head, and advanced toward me without the slightest hint of a bow; but there was more politeness in the openness and humanity of his expression than there is in the habit of drawing one leg behind the other, and of carrying in the hand what was made to cover the head.

"Friend," said he, "I see that thou art a stranger here; if I can be of any usefulness to thee, thou hast only to speak."

"Sir," said I, bending my body and sliding one foot toward him, according to our custom, "I flatter myself that my honest

[1] In a note added in 1739, Voltaire identifies the Quaker as Andrew Pitt (died at Hampstead, April 16, 1736). They were on good terms, though the Quaker complained that the account went beyond the truth, and assured Voltaire that God was offended at the fun made of the Quakers.

curiosity will not displease you, and that you will be so kind as to do me the honor of instructing me in your religion."

"The people of thy country," he replied, "make too many bows and compliments, but I have never yet seen one with such curiosity as thine. Come in, and let us first dine together."

I uttered a few more poor compliments, for one does not unmake one's habits all at once; and after a healthful and frugal repast which began and ended with a prayer to God, I set out interrogating my man. I began with the question that good Catholics have more than once asked of Huguenots: "My dear sir, have you been baptized?"

"No," said he, "and neither have my fellow Quakers."

"Zounds!" cried I. "Then you are not Christians?"

"My son," he answered gently, "do not swear. We are Christians and try to be good ones; but we do not think that Christianity consists in throwing cold water on the head, with a little seasoning."

"Good God!" cried I, outraged by this impiousness. "Have you forgotten, then, that Jesus Christ was baptized by John?"

"Friend," said the benign Quaker, "once more no swearing. Christ received baptism from John, but he baptized no one; we are the disciples not of John but of Christ."

"Gracious!" said I. "In an Inquisition country what a fire they would make of you, poor man. Do, for God's sake, let me baptize you and make a Christian out of you."

"If indulging thy weakness called only for that, we would do it willingly," was his grave answer. "We condemn no one for taking part in the ceremony of baptism, but we believe that those who profess a religion altogether holy and altogether spiritual must abstain as much as they can from Jewish rituals."

"That's a strange one," I exclaimed. "Jewish rituals?"

"Yes, my son," he continued, "and so much so that many Jews even today practice the baptism of John. Consult the ancient authors; they will teach thee that John only renewed an old practice which had been followed, among the Hebrews, long before his time, as the pilgrimage to Mecca had been among the Ishmaelites. Jesus consented to be baptized by John just as he submitted to circumcision, but circumcision and ceremonial washing were later to be done away with by the baptism of Christ, that baptism of the spirit, that ablution of the soul that saves mankind. Thus the forerunner John said, 'I indeed baptize you with water unto repentance: but he that cometh after me is mightier than I, whose shoes I am not worthy to bear: he shall baptize you with the Holy Ghost, and with fire.' [2] Thus the great apostle of the Gentiles, Paul, wrote to the Corinthians, 'Christ sent me not to baptize, but to preach the gospel.' [3] And Paul never did baptize any with water except two persons,[4] and that in spite of himself. He circumcised his disciple Timothy, and likewise the other apostles circumcised all who desired it. Art thou circumcised?" he added.

I replied that I had not had that honor.

"Very well, friend," said he, "thou art a Christian without being circumcised, and I without being baptized."

There was my holy man taking specious advantage of three or four passages of Holy Writ that seemed to favor his sect, and forgetting, in the best of faith, a hundred passages that crushed it. I took care not to dispute anything he said, for there's no arguing with an Enthusiast. Better not take it into one's head to tell a lover the faults of his mistress, or a litigant the weakness of his cause—or to talk sense to a fanatic. And so I went on to other questions.

"With regard to the communion," said I, "what are your customs?"

"We haven't any," said he.

"What, no communion?"

"No. None but the communion of hearts."

Once more he quoted Scripture. He made me a fine sermon against the communion, and took on a tone of inspiration in proving to me that all the sacraments were merely human in-

---

[2] Matthew 3:11.

[3] I Corinthians 1:17.

[4] Crispus and Gaius (I Cor. 1:14-15).

ventions, and that the word *sacrament* itself is not once to be found in the Gospel.

"Pardon my ignorance," he said. "I have not presented thee with a hundredth part of the proofs of my religion, but thou mayst find them in the exposition of our faith written by Robert Barclay,[5] one of the best books that ever came from the hand of man. Our enemies agree that it is highly dangerous, and that testifies to the honesty of its thought."

I promised to read this book, and my Quaker believed me already converted.

Later he explained to me briefly some of the peculiarities that expose this sect to the scorn of others.

"Confess," said he, "that it was all thou couldst do to keep from laughing when I replied to all thy courtesy in the second person singular and with my hat on. Yet thou seemst too well educated not to know that in the time of Christ no nation fell into the absurdity of substituting the plural for the singular. To Augustus Caesar one said, *I love thee, I beg thee, I thank thee;* he did not even allow anyone to call him Mister, *Dominus.* It was not till long after his day that people thought of addressing one another as *you* instead of *thou,* as if they came in pairs, and of usurping the impertinent titles of Lordship, Eminence, Holiness, which earthworms give to other earthworms in assuring them that they are, with profound respect and infamous falsity, their most humble and most obedient servants. It is in order to be more on our guard against this vile commerce of lies and flattery that we say *thou* to both kings and cobblers, and that we bow to no one, having nothing but kindness for men, and respect only for the laws.

"Our clothing too is a little different from that of other men, as a continual reminder to ourselves not to resemble

---

[5] Robert Barclay (1648-90), the great expositor of Quaker principles. His best known work is his "Apology." *Apology for the True Christian Divinity, as the same is set forth and preached by the people called in scorn Quakers:* such is the title of the 1678 English version of the work first published at Amsterdam (1676) as *Theologiae verae Christianae Apologia.*

them. Others wear the signs of their rank and dignity; we
wear those of Christian humility. We turn away from gay
parties, from shows, from gambling, for we should be much to
be pitied if we filled with such frivolity those hearts that God
should dwell in. We never swear, not even in court, feeling as
we do that the name of the Most High should not be bandied
about in the wretched contests of mankind. When it is necessary for us to appear before a magistrate in the affairs of
others (for we ourselves do not carry on lawsuits) we affirm
the truth with a *yes* or a *no,* and the judges accept our word,
though so many Christians forswear themselves on the very
Gospel. If we never go to war, it is not that we fear death—
on the contrary, we bless the moment that unites us with the
Being of Beings—but it's that we are not wolves or tigers or
watchdogs, but men and Christians. Our Lord, who has com-
manded us to love our enemies and to endure without com-
plaint, certainly does not wish us to cross the sea and cut the
throats of our brothers because some murderers dressed in red,
and wearing hats two feet high, are enlisting citizens by making a noise with two little sticks on the tightly stretched skin
of an ass. And when, after battles won, all London glitters
with lights, when the sky blazes with fireworks, and the air
resounds with the noise of thanksgiving, of bells, of organs,
and of cannon, we mourn in silence over these murders, the
cause of public gaiety."

LETTER TWO

ON THE QUAKERS

Such, in substance, was the conversation I had with that extraordinary man; but I was even more surprised when on the following Sunday he took me to the church of the Quakers. They have several chapels in London; the one I visited is near the famous pillar called the Monument. When I went in with my guide, the congregation had already assembled. There were about four hundred men in the church, and three hundred women; the women hid their faces with their fans, and the men were wearing their broad hats. All were seated, all in profound silence; I passed through the midst of them without causing a single person to look up at me. This silence lasted a quarter of an hour. Finally one of them rose, took off his hat, and after making some faces and heaving some sighs, began to intone, half through his mouth and half through his nose, a rigmarole which was taken, he thought, from the Gospel, and which was utterly meaningless to him and to everybody else. When this contortionist had finished his fine monologue, and the meeting had broken up with everyone both edified and in a stupor, I asked my companion why the more intelligent among them put up with such nonsense.

"We are obliged to tolerate it," he replied, "for it is impossible for us to know whether a man who rises to speak will be moved by the Spirit or by madness. Not knowing, we patiently listen to everything. We even allow women to speak. Often two or three of our devout females find themselves inspired at the same time, and then what a splendid noise there is in the house of the Lord!"

"Haven't you any priests?" I asked.

"No, friend," said the Quaker, "and we do very well with-

8

out them. God forbid that we should presume to ordain anyone to receive the Holy Ghost on Sunday to the exclusion of
the rest of the faithful. By God's grace we are the only ones
on earth to have no priests. Would you deprive us of so happy
a distinction? Why should we abandon our child to hired
nurses when we have milk of our own to give it? Those hirelings would soon dominate our household and tyrannize over
mother and child. Our Lord said, 'Freely ye have received;
freely give.' [1] Shall we, after this command, bargain for the
Gospel, put up the Holy Ghost for sale, and turn a Christian
meeting-place into a market? We do not give money to men
dressed in black to take care of our poor, bury our dead, and
preach to the faithful; these sacred duties are too dear to us
to be passed to the shoulders of others.

"But how can you tell," said I insistently, "whether it is
the Spirit of God that moves you in your speeches?"

"Whosoever prays that God enlighten him," he replied,
"and then declares the Gospel truths that move him, may be
sure that he has been inspired by God."

Whereupon he overwhelmed me with quotations from
Scripture proving, so he said, that there is no such thing as
Christianity without an immediate revelation. And he added
these remarkable words:

"When thou movest one of thy limbs, does thine own power
move it? Certainly not, for the same member often acts in-
voluntarily. It is He who created thy body, then, who gives
motion to this clay. And what of the ideas thy soul receives?
Is it thou who forms them? Even less so, for they come in
spite of thee. So it is the Creator of thy soul who gives thee
thine ideas. But as he has left thy heart free, he gives thy mind
such ideas as thy heart deserves. Thou livest in God; thou
actest, thou thinkest in God; and so thou hast only to open
thine eyes to that light which enlightens all men, and thou
shalt see the truth and make it to be seen."

"Ah, it's the purest Father Malebranche!" I exclaimed.

1 Matthew 10:8.

"I know thy Malebranche," said he. "He was a bit of a Quaker, but not enough of one." [2]

Those are the most important things I have learned about the doctrine of the Quakers. In the next letter you shall have their history, which you will find even more singular than their doctrine.

[2] Nicolas de Malebranche (1638-1715), member of the congregation of secular priests known as *l'Oratoire*. His philosophical system, which he condensed in his *Entretiens sur la métaphysique et la religion* (1687) was started on its way by his study of Descartes. To him, human reason and the Divine Word are one; we see all things in God, and are unable to move except through the action of the divine upon us.

LETTER THREE

ON THE QUAKERS

You have already seen that the Quakers date from Jesus Christ, who was, according to them, the first Quaker.[1] Religion, they say, was corrupted almost immediately after his death, and remained in corruption some sixteen hundred years; but there were always a few Quakers hidden away in the world, who carefully fostered the sacred flame that was extinct wherever they were not, until finally the light spread to England in the year 1642.[2]

It was in the days when three or four sects were tearing Great Britain apart with wars undertaken in the name of God, that one George Fox, of the county of Leicester, son of a silk-weaver, took it into his head to preach like a true Apostle, according to him—that is, without knowing how to read or write.[3] He was a young man of twenty-five, of irreproachable habits, and mad in a saintly way. Clothed in leather from head to foot, he went from village to village, shouting against war and the clergy. If he had only preached against the military, he would have had nothing to fear; but he attacked churchmen: he was promptly sent to prison. When they led him be-

[1] Voltaire's main source of information for this chapter is William Sewel, *The History of the Rise, Increase, and Progress of the Christian People Called Quakers* (1722). He makes some borrowings from Gerard Croese, *Historia Quakeriana* (1695), and he may have seen William Penn's *A Brief Account of the Rise and Progress of the People Called Quakers* (1694).

[2] Fox was born in 1624. In order for him to be twenty-five (see below), 1642 would have to be changed to 1649.

[3] He appears to have known at least how to read at that age; he never wrote like one of the learned, though in all he said he drew heavily on Scripture.

11

fore the justice of the peace at Derby, he presented himself with his leather cap on his head. An officer gave him a smart box on the ear, saying,

"You beggar, don't you know enough to be bareheaded in the presence of his honor?"

Fox turned the other cheek, and begged the officer to hit him again for the love of God. The Derby justice tried to get him to take oath before being questioned.

"Friend," said he to the justice, "thou must know that I never take the name of the Lord in vain."

Hearing himself *thee'd* and *thou'd* by this man, the justice sent him to the Bedlam of Derby to be whipped. Praising God along the way, George Fox went to his lunatic asylum, where the sentence of the magistrate was rigorously carried out.[4] Those who inflicted on him the penance of the whip were much surprised when he begged them to flog him some more with a birch for the good of his soul. These gentlemen needed no begging, and Fox had his double dose, for which he thanked them cordially. He began to preach to them; first they laughed, then they listened, and, since the disease of Enthusiasm is catching, several were converted, and those who had whipped him became his first disciples.

Released from prison, he wandered about the country with a dozen proselytes, still preaching against the clergy, and having himself whipped from time to time. One day, having been set in the pillory,[5] he harangued the crowd so forcefully that he converted some fifty of his audience, and roused so much sympathy in the others that they freed him uproar-

[4] Fox was sent to a house of correction for blasphemy, as if for a kind of disorderly conduct. In the same place might be found vagrants, idlers, rogues, the infirm, and the mad. Voltaire has no trouble in turning "house of correction" into "the *Petites-Maisons* of Derby," and then—because in the Hospice des Petites-Maisons in Paris lunatics as well as beggars were lodged—into "*l'Hôpital des Fous.*"

[5] Voltaire probably invented the instance of Fox in the pillory, piecing it together from other stories.

iously, sought out the Anglican clergyman through whose influence Fox had been condemned to stand, and pilloried him in his place.

He had the cheek to convert some of Cromwell's soldiers, whereupon they quit the service and refused to take the oath.[6] Cromwell wanted nothing to do with a sect whose members would not fight, as Sixtus the Fifth augured ill of a sect *dove non si chiavava.*[7] He took advantage of his power to persecute these newcomers; the prisons were filled with them. But persecution seldom has any other effect than to make new proselytes; they emerged from prison confirmed in their belief and followed by their jailers, whom they had converted. But here is what contributed most to the increase of the sect: Fox believed himself inspired. The consequence was that he thought he should speak in a different way from other men; he began to tremble, to contort his body and make wry faces, to hold his breath, and then to expel it violently. The Priestess of Delphi wouldn't have made a better job of it. In a short time, inspiration had become remarkably habitual with him, and soon afterward it was almost impossible for him to hold forth in any other way. This was the first gift he bestowed upon his disciples. With perfect sincerity, they made all the grimaces their Master did; they trembled as hard as they could in the moment of inspiration. Hence the name of Quakers. The crowd amused themselves with mimicking them. People trembled, talked through their noses, had convulsions, and fancied that the Holy Ghost was in them.

A few miracles seemed called for; they performed them.

Said the Patriarch Fox to a justice of the peace, before a large audience, "Friend, take care: God will soon punish thee for persecuting the Saints." This justice was a drunkard who

---

[6] At the beginning of 1654 Cromwell required of his soldiers an oath of fidelity. Refusing to take the oath, then, would seem to come first here.

[7] "where there was no sexual intercourse." One of the bulls of Pope Sixtus the Fifth (1521-90) forbade eunuchs to marry.

every day drank altogether too much bad beer and brandy; he died of apoplexy two days after the warning, at the precise moment that he finished signing an order committing some Quakers to prison.[8] The sudden death of the justice was in no way attributed to his intemperance; everyone regarded it as an effect of the holy man's predictions.

That death made more Quakers than a thousand sermons and as many convulsions could have done. Cromwell, seeing that their number increased every day, wished to entice them into his party. He had them offered money, but they were incorruptible, and he said one day that theirs was the sole religion against which guineas had not enabled him to prevail.

They were sometimes persecuted under Charles II, not for their religion, but for refusing to pay tithes, for *theeing* and *thouing* magistrates, and refusing to take oath as prescribed by law.

At last, Robert Barclay, a Scot, presented to the King, in 1675, his *Apology* for the Quakers, as good a work as it could be. The dedication to Charles II contains, not base flattery, but bold truths and good counsel.

"Thou hast tasted of prosperity and adversity," he says to Charles at the end of this epistle; "thou knowest what it is to be banished thy native country, to be overruled, as well as to rule, and sit upon the throne; and being *oppressed*, thou hast reason to know how *hateful* the *oppressor* is both to God and man: If after all these warnings and advertisements, thou dost not turn unto the Lord with all thy heart, but forget him, who remembered thee in thy distress, and give up thyself to follow lust and vanity; surely great will be thy condemnation.

"Against which snare as well as the temptation of those that may or do feed thee, and prompt thee to evil, the most excellent and prevalent remedy will be, to apply thyself to that *Light of Christ,* which *shineth in thy conscience,* which neither can nor will flatter thee, nor suffer thee to be at ease

---

[8] Voltaire's art has improved upon nature.

in thy sins; but doth and will deal plainly and faithfully with thee, as those that are followers thereof have also done.

     . . . Thy faithful friend and subject,

       Robert Barclay." [9]

Yet more astonishing: this letter written to a King by an obscure private citizen had its effect and the persecution ceased.

[9] Barclay's English version of the *Apology* (pp. viii-ix, second stereotype edition, from the eighth London edition: New York, 1827). Voltaire has sensibly condensed the last paragraph. Here is his French version:

Tu as goûté, dit-il à Charles à la fin de cette Épître, de la douceur et de l'amertume, de la prospérité et des plus grands malheurs; tu as été chassé des pays où tu règnes; tu as senti le poids de l'oppression, et tu dois savoir combien l'oppresseur est détestable devant Dieu et devant les hommes. Que si, après tant d'épreuves et de bénédictions, ton coeur s'endurcissait et oubliait le Dieu qui s'est souvenu de toi dans tes disgrâces, ton crime en serait plus grand et ta condamnation plus terrible. Au lieu donc d'écouter les flatteurs de ta Cour, écoute la voix de ta conscience, qui ne te flattera jamais. Je suis ton fidèle ami et sujet BARCLAY.

ON THE QUAKERS · 15

LETTER FOUR

ON THE QUAKERS

About this time there appeared on the scene the illustrious
William Penn, who established the power of the Quakers in
America, and who would have secured them respectability in
Europe if men were able to respect virtue when it lies beneath
a ridiculous exterior. He was the only son of Vice-Admiral
Penn, a favorite of the Duke of York who was later James II.

At the age of fifteen, William Penn met a Quaker at Oxford, where he was studying at the time. This Quaker made
a proselyte of him, and the young man, who was lively and
naturally eloquent, and had a certain nobility of feature and
of manners, soon won over certain of his fellow students.
There quietly grew up a society of young Quakers who met
together at his rooms; so that at the age of sixteen he found
himself at the head of a sect.

On his return home after leaving college, instead of kneel-
ing before the Vice-Admiral his father and asking his blessing
according to English custom, he confronted him with his hat
on, and said to him, "I am happy, friend, to see thee in good
health." The Vice-Admiral thought his son had gone mad,
and then realized that he had become a Quaker. He used every
means available to human prudence in order to induce him to
live like other people. The young man's only reply was to ex-
hort his father to become a Quaker himself.

At last the father gave way so far as to ask no more than
that he wait upon the King and the Duke of York with his
hat under his arm, and without *theeing* and *thouing* them.
William replied that his conscience would not permit it, and
his father, in indignation and despair, drove him from the
house. Young Penn gave thanks to God that he was already

suffering in His cause, went to preach in the City, and made
a large number of converts.

The sermons of the ministers grew more enlightening every
day, and as Penn was young, handsome, and well made, the
women of both court and town devotedly flocked to hear him.
The Patriarch, George Fox, came from the other end of England to London to see him, on the strength of his reputation,
and the two resolved to do missionary work in foreign countries. They embarked for Holland, having left behind them
workers in sufficient numbers to take care of the London vine-
yard. Their labors had happy results in Amsterdam, but what
redounded most to their honor, and put their humility most
in danger, was the reception given them by Elizabeth, Princess
Palatine, aunt of King George I of England, a woman renowned for her intelligence and her knowledge, to whom
Descartes had dedicated his novel about philosophy.[1]

She was then living a retired life at the Hague,[2] where she
welcomed these *friends*—for so the Quakers were called in
Holland at that time.[3] She had several discussions with them,
they often preached to her household, and if they did not
make a perfect Quakeress of her, they allowed at least that
she was not far from the Kingdom of Heaven.

The Friends sowed in Germany too, but they reaped little.
There was no taste for the fashion of *theeing* and *thouing* in
a country where one must always have on the tip of the
tongue such words as *Highness* and *Excellency*. Penn soon

[1] Elizabeth of Bohemia, Princess Palatine (1618-80), eldest daughter of
Elizabeth "Queen of Hearts" and Frederick V. In 1667 she acquired and
became abbess of the Lutheran monastery at Herford in old Westphalia,
and turned it into the first school of Cartesianism. Her interest in the
mystical attracted the attention of Quaker missionaries, among them
Barclay, Penn, and Fox (Fox did not go to Herford). The visit described
by Voltaire was in 1677; in 1644 her friend and correspondent Descartes
had dedicated to her his *Principia Philosophiae*. Soon afterward he wrote
his treatise on the passions (*Les Passions de l'Ame*) to meet certain of her
objections to his thought. (See also Letter XIV, note 2.)

[2] Herford, rather.

[3] In England as well, of course.

returned to England, having heard that his father was ill, and wishing to be with him in his last moments. The Vice-Admiral was reconciled with him, and embraced him tenderly even though he was of a different religion. William vainly exhorted his father not to receive the sacrament and to die a Quaker, and the old fellow fruitlessly advised William to wear buttons on his sleeves and ribbons on his hat.

William inherited great possessions, among them debts of the Crown for sums the Vice-Admiral had advanced for naval expeditions. Nothing was less certain at the time than money owed by the King; Penn was obliged more than once to go and *thee* and *thou* Charles II and his ministers for what was owing him. In 1680 the government gave him, in place of money, the ownership and sovereignty of a province in America south of Maryland. So now a Quaker had become a sovereign. He left for his new estates followed by two vessels loaded with Quakers.

From that time on, those lands have been called Pennsylvania, after him. He founded there the city of Philadelphia, today a very flourishing one. He began by making an alliance with the Americans, his neighbors. This is the only treaty between these peoples and the Christians that was never sworn to and has never been broken. The new sovereign was also the legislator of Pennsylvania; he enacted wise laws, none of which has since been altered. The first is to mistreat no one for his religion, and to regard all those who believe in a God as brothers.

Hardly had he established his government, when a number of American merchants arrived to people this colony. The natives of the country, instead of fleeing into the forests, gradually got used to the peaceable Quakers; to the degree that they hated the other Christians, conquerors and destroyers of America, they loved these newcomers. Before long, delighted with the gentleness of their neighbors, a great crowd of these supposed savages came to ask William Penn if he would receive them as his vassals. It was quite a new sort of spectacle: a sovereign whom everyone familiarly *thee'd* and *thou'd,* and spoke to with one's hat on; a government without priests, a people without weapons, citizens all of them equals —magistrates excepted—and neighbors free from jealousy.[4]

William Penn could boast of having brought forth on this earth the Golden Age that everyone talks so much about, and that probably never was, except in Pennsylvania. After the death of Charles II, he returned to England on business for his new country. King James, who had loved the father, had the same affection for the son, and considered him no longer as an obscure sectary but as a very great man. The politics of the King agreed, in this respect, with his own in-clinations. He had a mind to please the Quakers by abolish-ing the laws against nonconformists, so as quietly, under cover of liberty, to bring Roman Catholicism in. All the sects in England saw the trap and took care not to be caught in it. They are always united against Catholicism, their common enemy; but Penn did not believe himself obliged to renounce his principles and take the part of Protestants who hated him against a King who loved him. He had established liberty of conscience in America; he had no desire to look as if he were destroying it in Europe. He therefore remained faithful to James II, so much so that he was generally accused of being a

---

[4] The Constitution of Pennsylvania, drawn up by Penn, was the first to guarantee liberty of conscience, though within limits that were taken for granted.

"35th: That all persons living in this province, who confess and ac-knowledge the one almighty and eternal God, to be the creator, upholder, and ruler of the world, and that hold themselves obliged in conscience to live peaceably and justly in civil society, shall in no ways be molested or prejudiced for their religious persuasion or practice in matters of faith and worship, nor shall they be compelled at any time to frequent or maintain any religious worship place or ministry whatever."—Penn's *First Frame of Government,* 1682.

Officials of various sorts had to profess faith in Jesus Christ. The Lord's Day was to be kept. There was "discouragement" and severe punishment of drunkenness, uncleanness, duels, stage plays, cards, dice, May-games, masques, revels, cockfighting, etc.

Jesuit. This calumny wounded him deeply, and he felt it necessary to justify himself in print. However, the unfortunate James II, who like almost all the Stuarts was a mixture of greatness and weakness, and who like them did both too much and too little, lost his kingdom without one's being able to say quite how it happened.

All the English sects accepted from William III and his parliament the same liberty they had been unwilling to owe to James. It was then that the Quakers began, by force of law, to enjoy all the privileges they are in possession of today. Penn, after having seen his sect at last firmly established in the land of his birth, returned to Pennsylvania. His own people and the Americans welcomed him with tears of joy as a father who had come home to his children. All his laws had been religiously observed during his absence—something that never happened to any legislator before him. He remained in Philadelphia for a number of years and departed at last, reluctantly, to solicit in London some new commercial advantages for the Pennsylvanians. He lived in London from that time on into extreme old age, looked upon as the head of a people and of a religion. He did not die till 1718.

The ownership and government were reserved to his descendants, who sold the latter to the Crown for £12,000. The circumstances of the King permitted him to pay no more than a thousand. A French reader will perhaps expect that the ministry paid the rest in promises, and meanwhile took over the government. Not at all: since the Crown had been unable to complete payment within the prescribed time, the contract was declared void, and the Penn family resumed its rights.

I cannot guess at the future of the Quaker religion in America, but I see it daily declining in London. In every country the dominant religion, if it does not actually persecute all the others, swallows them up in the end. Quakers cannot be members of Parliament, nor can they hold office, for in either case one must take oath,[5] and they refuse to

———
[5] In 1696 an act was passed to accept the Quakers' "solemn affirmation and declaration . . . instead of an oath in the usual form." These are the

swear. They are reduced to making money by means of commerce. The children, made rich by the industry of their fathers, want to enjoy themselves, to acquire honors, buttons, and cuffs. They are ashamed to be called Quakers, and are turning Anglican to be in style.

---

words they were to use: "I, A. B., do declare in the presence of Almighty God, the witness of the truth of what I say. . . ." They remained unqualified to give evidence in criminal causes, or serve on juries, or "bear any office or place of profit in the government."

LETTER FIVE

ON THE CHURCH OF ENGLAND

This is the country of sects. An Englishman, as a free man, goes to Heaven by whatever road he pleases.

Yet, though everyone here may serve God in his own fashion, their genuine Religion, the one in which people make their fortune, is the sect of Episcopalians, called the Church of England, or pre-eminently The Church. No one can hold office in England or in Ireland unless he is a faithful Anglican.[1] This argument, in itself a convincing proof, has converted so many nonconformists that today not a twentieth of the population lives outside the lap of the established Church.

The Anglican clergy has retained many of the Catholic ceremonies, particularly that of gathering in tithes with the most scrupulous attention. They also have the pious ambition of being the Masters.

Moreover, they work up in their flocks as much holy zeal against nonconformists as possible. This zeal was lively enough under the government of the Tories in the last years of Queen Anne, but it went no further than sometimes breaking the windows of heretical chapels; for the fury of the sects was over, in England, with the civil wars, and under Queen Anne nothing was left but the restless noises of a sea still heaving a long time after the storm. When Whigs and Tories were

---

[1] The Test Act of 1673 supported the Corporation Act (1661: obligation of magistrates to receive the sacrament in the Church of England), and the Act of Uniformity (1662: complete acceptance of the Book of Common Prayer by clergymen and teachers), by forbidding the holding of public office to those who refused to receive the sacrament in the Church of England and to deny transubstantiation. James II defied the Test Act by appointing Roman Catholics to office. This was political and religious subversion that aroused most Englishmen and gratified Louis XIV.

rending their native land as Guelphs and Ghibellines once had done, it was of course necessary that religion should become a party issue. The Tories were for episcopacy, the Whigs wanted to abolish it—but when they were on top they were content to humble it.

In the days when Harley, Earl of Oxford, and Lord Bolingbroke were having people drink the health of the Tories, the Church of England looked upon them as the defenders of its holy privileges. The lower house of convocation, which is a sort of house of commons made up of clergymen, had then some importance; at least they enjoyed the liberty of meeting, of arguing controversial points, and of now and then burning a few impious books—that is, books written against them. The ministry, which is a Whig one nowadays, does not even allow these gentlemen to hold their convocation; they are reduced, in the obscurity of their parishes, to the sad occupation of praying for a government they would not be sorry to distress. As for the bishops, who are twenty-six in all, they sit in the House of Lords in spite of the Whigs, for the old abuse of considering them the equivalent of barons still subsists; but they have no more power in the House than the ducal peers in the Parliament of Paris.

There is a clause in the oath that one must take to the state that sorely tries the Christian patience of these gentlemen: this is one's promise to be of the Church as it was established by law. There is hardly a bishop, a dean, an archdeacon, who does not think he holds his position by divine right; it is therefore highly mortifying to them to have to acknowledge that they owe everything to a miserable law made by profane laymen. A monk (Father Courayer) recently wrote a book to confirm the validity and the succession of ordinations in the Church of England.[2] This work was condemned in France, but do you think it pleased the English ministry? Not in the least. It's of very little concern to these cursed Whigs whether the succession of bishops has been interrupted in their country or not, and whether Bishop

---

[2] *Dissertation sur la validité des ordinations Anglicanes et sur la succession des Evesques de l'Eglise Anglicane*, (Brussels, 1723).

Parker was consecrated in a tavern (as it is rumored) or in a church. They prefer that bishops derive their authority from parliament rather than from the Apostles. Lord B.[3] says that this concept of divine right can only make tyrants in miters,[4] but that citizens are made by the law.

With regard to morals, the Anglican clergy are better ordered than those of France, and this is the reason: all clergymen are brought up in Oxford University, or in Cambridge, far from the corruption of the capital. They are not called to high station in the Church until very late, and at an age when men have no other passion but avarice, if their ambition goes unfed. Positions of rank are here the reward of long service in the Church just as in the army; one does not see young fellows made bishops or colonels on leaving school. Besides, the priests are almost all married; the awkwardness they pick up in the university, and the fact that, socially, Englishmen have little to do with women, result in a bishop's ordinarily being forced to content himself with his own wife. Clergymen go to the tavern sometimes, for custom allows it; if they get drunk they do so in a serious-minded way and with perfect propriety.

That indefinable being which is neither ecclesiastical nor secular—in a word, that which is called an *Abbé*—is a species unknown in England. Clergymen here are all reserved, by temperament, and almost all pedantic. When they learn that in France young men, who are known for their debauchery and who have been raised to the prelacy by the plots of women, make love in public, divert themselves with the composing of sentimental songs, entertain daily with long and exquisite supper parties, and go from there to beseech the light of the Holy Spirit, and boldly to call themselves the successors of the Apostles—then the English thank God they are Protestants. But they are nasty heretics, fit to be burned to Hell and back, as Master François Rabelais says. That's why I keep out of it.

3 Sufficiently characteristic of Bolingbroke.
4 Or camails and rochets, if the reader pleases.

LETTER SIX

ON THE PRESBYTERIANS

The Church of England is confined to England and Ireland. Presbyterianism is the predominant religion in Scotland. This Presbyterianism is nothing other than the purest Calvinism, as Calvinism was when it was established in France, and as it still is in Geneva. As the priests of this sect receive from their churches none but the meanest wages, and as consequently they are unable to live in the same luxury as bishops, they have taken the natural course of inveighing against a dignity they cannot attain to. Imagine the proud Diogenes treading under his feet the pride of Plato: the Presbyterians of Scotland are not unlike that arrogant and beggarly dialectician. They treated King Charles II with a good deal less respect than Diogenes treated Alexander. For when they took up arms for him against Cromwell, who had deceived them, they made this poor king undergo four sermons a day, they forbade him to gamble, they made him stand in the corner—so that Charles was soon weary of being king of such pedants, and escaped as a boy slips away from school.

Compared with a young and lively French theological student, squalling at the university in the morning and singing with the ladies at night, an Anglican theologue is a Cato; but this Cato looks like a regular man-about-town if you set him beside a Scotch Presbyterian. The latter affects a solemn bearing, an air of displeasure; he wears a huge hat and a long cloak over a short coat, preaches through his nose, and gives the title of Whore of Babylon to all churches in which some of the clergy are fortunate enough to have an income of fifty thousand pounds, and where the people are so kind as to suffer it and call them My Lord, Your Grace, or Your Eminence.

25

These gentlemen, who also have some churches in England, have made grave airs and severe expressions all the fashion in this country. To them is owing the sanctification of Sunday in the three kingdoms. On that day it is forbidden to work and play, which is double the severity of the Catholic churches. No opera, no plays, no concerts in London on Sunday; even cards are so expressly forbidden that only the aristocracy, and those we call well-bred people, play on that day. The rest of the nation go to church, to the tavern, and to the brothel.

Although the Episcopalian and the Presbyterian are the two main sects in Great Britain, all others are welcome there and live pretty comfortably together, though most of their preachers detest one another almost as cordially as a Jansenist damns a Jesuit.

Go into the Exchange in London, that place more venerable than many a court, and you will see representatives of all the nations assembled there for the profit of mankind. There the Jew, the Mahometan, and the Christian deal with one another as if they were of the same religion, and reserve the name of infidel for those who go bankrupt. There the Presbyterian trusts the Anabaptist, and the Church of England man accepts the promise of the Quaker. On leaving these peaceable and free assemblies, some go to the synagogue, others in search of a drink; this man is on the way to be baptized in a great tub in the name of the Father, by the Son, to the Holy Ghost; that man is having the foreskin of his son cut off, and a Hebraic formula mumbled over the child that he himself can make nothing of; these others are going to their church to await the inspiration of God with their hats on; and all are satisfied.

If there were only one religion in England, there would be danger of tyranny; if there were two, they would cut each other's throats; but there are thirty, and they live happily together in peace.

LETTER SEVEN

ON THE SOCINIANS, OR ARIANS, OR ANTI-TRINITARIANS

There is a little sect here composed of clergymen and of a few very learned laymen, who do not call themselves Arians, or Socinians either, but who are by no means of the opinion of St. Athanasius on the matter of the Trinity, and will tell you plainly that the Father is greater than the Son.

You remember hearing about a certain Orthodox bishop who, in order to convince an emperor of the truth of consubstantiation, ventured to take the emperor's son by the chin and pull his nose in the presence of His Sacred Majesty. The emperor was about to get angry with the bishop, when the good man delivered to him these fine and persuasive words: "My lord emperor, if your majesty is angry that a lack of respect has been shown your son, how do you suppose God the Father will behave toward those who refuse to Jesus Christ the titles that are his due?" The people I am discussing say that the holy bishop was most ill advised, that his argument was far from conclusive, and that the emperor ought to have replied to him, "Learn that there are two ways to be lacking in respect for me: first, in failing to pay sufficient honor to my son; second, in paying him as much as you do to me."

However that may be, the party of Arius is beginning to revive in England as well as in Holland and Poland. The great Mr. Newton did its doctrine the honor of favoring it; that philosopher thought the Unitarians reasoned more geometrically than we. But the strongest patron of the Arian

27

doctrine is the famous Doctor Clarke. This is a man of rigid virtue and gentle disposition, more fond of his ideas than desirous of propagating them, wholly taken up with calculations and demonstrations: a veritable reasoning-machine.

It is he who is the author of a book, rather little understood but highly esteemed, on the existence of God, and of another, more intelligible but looked upon with some contempt, on the truth of the Christian religion.

He has not engaged in any splendid scholastic disputes, such as our friend . . .[1] calls *venerable humbug;* he has been content to publish a book containing all the testimony of the first centuries for and against the Unitarians, and left it to the reader to count the votes and pass sentence. This book of the Doctor's has won him many adherents but has prevented him from being Archbishop of Canterbury. I believe the Doctor made a mistake in his calculations, and that it is better to be an English Primate than an Arian curate.

See what revolutions occur in realms of opinion as well as in empires. The party of Arius, after three hundred years of triumph and twelve centuries of oblivion, is reborn at last from its ashes. But it has chosen its time very badly, to reappear in an age when the world is satiated with controversies and with sects. This one is still too small to obtain the liberty of holding public assemblies; it will obtain it, no doubt, if its numbers increase; but people are so lukewarm about all such matters nowadays that there is hardly a chance any more for a new or renovated religion to make its fortune. Isn't it amusing that Luther, Calvin, Zwingli, all of them unreadable writers, should have founded sects that portion out Europe among themselves; that the ignorant Mahomet should have given a religion to Asia and Africa; and that Messrs. Newton, Clarke, Locke, Leclerc, *et al.,* the greatest philosophers and the best writers of their time, should just barely have managed to acquire a little flock of followers that, small as it is, dwindles every day?

[1] Rabelais? Bolingbroke? Voltaire himself?

That is what it means to come into the world at the right time. If Cardinal de Retz reappeared today, he would not be able to rouse up ten women in all Paris.

If Cromwell were born again, he who once had the head of his king cut off, and who made himself a sovereign, would be a plain London tradesman.

LETTER EIGHT

ON THE PARLIAMENT

The members of the Parliament of England are fond of comparing themselves to the ancient Romans whenever the occasion arises.

Not long ago Mr. Shippen [1] began a speech in the House of Commons with these words: "The majesty of the English people would be wounded. . . ." The oddness of this expression raised a great shout of laughter; but without embarrassment Mr. Shippen repeated his words firmly, and the House was quiet. I confess that I see no resemblance between the majesty of the English people and that of the Roman, and even less between their governments. There is a senate in London, some of whose members are under suspicion, doubtless unjustly, of selling their votes on occasion, as was done in Rome: this is the only similarity. Otherwise, the two nations seem to me quite different as to both good and evil. Among the Romans the horrible madness of religious wars was unknown; that abomination was reserved for pious preachers of humility and patience. Marius and Sulla, Pompey and Caesar, Antony and Augustus did not fight over the question whether the Flamen should wear his shirt over his robe or his robe over his shirt; or whether, for auspices to be taken, the sacred chickens must both eat and drink or simply eat.[2] The English have in the past reciprocally hanged one another at their Assizes and destroyed one another in pitched battle over matters of this kind. Episcopalianism and Presbyterianism have turned these grave heads for a time. I suppose that no such foolishness will get control of them again, however, for

[1] A Tory and Jacobite, adversary of Walpole.

[2] It was by the appetite of these birds that the augurs interpreted the divine will.

they appear to me to have grown wiser at their own expense, and I see in them no longer any inclination to cut one another's throats over syllogisms.

There is a more essential difference between Rome and England which gives all the advantage to the latter, and that is that in Rome the fruit of civil wars was slavery, whereas in England it was freedom. The English are the only people on earth who have managed to prescribe limits to the power of kings by resisting them, and who by long endeavor have at last established that wise form of government in which the prince, all-powerful to do good, is restrained from doing evil; [3] in which the nobles are great without insolence or feudal power, and the people take part in the government without disorder.

The House of Lords and that of the Commons are the arbiters of the nation, and the king is umpire. This balance the Romans lacked; there was always discord in Rome between the nobles and the common people, and no intermediary with power to reconcile them. The Senate of Rome, which had the unjust, the criminal arrogance to refuse to share anything with the plebeians, knew no other trick for keeping government out of their reach than to busy them continually with foreign wars. They regarded the People as a ferocious animal that had better be let loose upon the neighbors than kept at home to devour its master. Thus the greatest weakness in the government of the Romans made conquerors of them; it is because they were unhappy at home that they became the masters of the world—until domestic discord turned them into slaves.

The government of England was not made for such a burst of grandeur, nor for so disastrous an end. Its purpose is not the splendid folly of making conquests but to prevent its neighbors from making them. This people is not only jealous of its liberty, it is at the same time concerned about the liberty

[3] See Fénelon's *Télémaque* (Book V), where the old Cretan is defining the royal authority. Voltaire has borrowed this particular antithesis almost word for word.

of others. The English were implacably opposed to Louis XIV for the sole reason that they thought him ambitious. They waged war against him with a light heart and surely without self-interest.

It has doubtless cost a good deal to establish liberty in England; the idol of arbitrary power was drowned in seas of blood. But the English do not believe that for good laws too high a price has been paid. Other nations have not had fewer troubles nor poured out less blood, but the blood they shed for liberty has only hardened their bondage.

What becomes a revolution in England is only a mutiny in other countries. In Spain, in Barbary, or in Turkey a city will take to arms to defend its privileges, and immediately it is subjugated by mercenary soldiers, and punished by executioners, and the rest of the nation kisses its chains. The French think that the government of this island is stormier than the sea that surrounds it, and so it is; but that is when the king provokes the tempest, when he wants to make himself master of the ship of which he is only the pilot. The civil wars of France have been longer, more ruthless, more productive of crimes than those of England, but not one of all these civil wars had a wise liberty for its object.

In the detestable days of Charles IX and Henri III the only question was whether one was going to be the slave of the Guise family. As for the last war of Paris, it deserves only catcalls. I seem to see a crowd of schoolboys rioting against their headmaster, and being whipped for it. Cardinal de Retz, a man who had much wit and courage and used them badly, a rebel without a cause, a dissident without a plan, head of a faction without an army, intrigued for the sake of intrigue, and seemed to foment civil war for his own pleasure. The Parlement knew neither what it had in mind nor what it didn't have in mind. It raised troops by decree and discharged them; it threatened, it apologized; it put a price on the head of Cardinal Mazarin and then came to compliment him in state. Our civil wars under Charles VI had been savage; those of the Ligue were abominable; that of the Fronde was ridiculous.

What the French chiefly reproach the English for is the execution of Charles I, who was treated by his vanquishers as he would have treated them if he had been lucky.

After all, consider on the one hand Charles I defeated in pitched battle, made prisoner, tried, sentenced at Westminster; and on the other hand the emperor Henry VII [4] poisoned by his chaplain while receiving the sacrament; Henri III killed by a monk, minister to the fury of a whole faction; thirty plots to assassinate Henri IV, several set going, and the last one depriving France of that great king forever. Weigh these outrages, and then judge.

[4] Thirty-first Holy Roman Emperor; of the house of Luxembourg, he died near Siena in 1913. The crime, as Voltaire says in *Annals of the Empire,* is difficult to prove. But that does little harm to the argument.

LETTER NINE

ON THE GOVERNMENT

This happy mixture in the government of England, this union of commons, lords, and king, has not always been in effect. England was long a slave; it was enslaved to the Romans, the Saxons, the Danes, the French. William the Conqueror, more than others, governed with an iron scepter; he disposed of the property and the life of his new subjects like some Oriental monarch. He forbade, on pain of death, any Englishman to be so presumptuous as to have any fire or light in his house after eight in the evening—either expecting by such measures to prevent their assembling at night, or else wishing to discover, by so bizarre a prohibition, just how far the power of one man over other men could go.

It is true that before and after William the Conqueror the English had parliaments; they boast about it, as if the assemblies then called parliaments, composed as they were of ecclesiastical tyrants and of plunderers known as barons—as if those assemblies were the guardians of liberty and public bliss.

The barbarians, who from the shores of the Baltic Sea poured into the rest of Europe, brought with them the custom of these legislative bodies or parliaments that so much fuss is made about and are so little known. The kings at the time were not despotic, it is true, but the people only groaned the more for it in a wretched state of bondage. The chiefs of these savages who had devastated France, Italy, Spain, and England made themselves kings; their captains shared among themselves the lands of the conquered: hence these margraves, these lairds, these barons, these under-tyrants who often squabbled with their king over what they had plundered from the peoples. They were birds of prey battling an eagle to suck

the blood of doves. Each people had a hundred tyrants instead of one master. The priests soon joined the party. It had
always been the fate of the Gauls, the Germans, and the
islanders of England to be ruled by their druids and by the
chiefs of their villages, an ancient species of baron, less
tyrannical than what came after. These druids professed to be
mediators between the deity and mankind; they made laws,
they excommunicated people, they condemned people to
death. The bishops gradually succeeded to their temporal
authority in the Goth and Vandal governments. The popes
put themselves at the head of them, and with breves, bulls,
and monks, made kings tremble, deposed them, had them
assassinated, and drew to themselves as much of the money of
Europe as they could. The imbecile Ina, one of the tyrants of
the English Heptarchy, was the first who on a pilgrimage to
Rome consented to pay Peter pence (which would amount to
about an *écu* in our money) for every house in his lands. The
whole island promptly followed his example, England little
by little became a province of the pope, and the Holy Father
sent his legates there from time to time to levy exorbitant
taxes. At last, John Lackland, following regulations, ceded
his realm to His Holiness, who had excommunicated him;
and the barons, who found that not exactly to their interest,
drove out their miserable king. They put in his place Louis
VIII, the father of St. Louis of France, but they soon sickened
of this newcomer and sent him back across the water.

While barons, bishops, and popes were in this way pulling
apart an England of which they all wanted control, the people,
the most numerous, the most virtuous even, and consequently
the most respectable class of men, composed of those who
devote themselves to the laws and the sciences, of merchants,
of craftsmen—in a word, of all that was not tyrannical—the
people, I say, were regarded by them as animals on a plane
below the human. The commons were then far from having
any part in the government; they were villeins: their labor,
their blood belonged to their masters, who were called nobles.
Most men were, throughout Europe then, what they still are

in several parts of the North, serfs of a lord, a species of cattle bought and sold with the land. It has taken centuries to do justice to humanity, to feel it was horrible that the many should sow and the few should reap. And isn't it a good thing for the human race that the authority of those little brigands was stamped out in France by the legitimate power of our kings, and in England by the legitimate power of the kings and the people?

Fortunately, in the shaking that the strife between kings and nobles gave to empires, the chains of the nations have been more or less loosened. Liberty was born in England of the quarrels between tyrants. The barons forced John Lackland and Henry III to grant that famous Charter whose main purpose was really to make the kings subordinate to the lords, but in which the rest of the nation was favored a little, so that when the occasion arose they would range themselves on the side of their pretended protectors. That Great Charter, which is regarded as the consecrated source of English liberty, shows very clearly in itself how little liberty was known. The title alone proves that the King thought himself absolute by right, and that the barons and even the clergy were able to force him to relax his hold on this pretended right only by being stronger than he.

This is how the Great Charter begins: "We grant of our own free will the following rights to archbishops, bishops, abbots, priors, and barons of our realm," etc.[1]

In the articles of that Charter not a word is said about the House of Commons, which is proof that it did not yet exist, or that it existed in impotence. The "freemen" of England are specified there, sad evidence that there were some who were not that. It is clear by Article 32 that these supposedly free men owed services to their lord. Such liberty had a remarkable resemblance to slavery.

In Article 21 the king orders that his officers no longer be permitted to seize by force the horses and carts of free men

[1] Voltaire's information about the charter comes from the condensation of Rapin de Thoyras.

unless payment is made, and this regulation struck the people as true liberty, because it removed a greater kind of tyranny.

Henry VII, a successful usurper and great politician, who pretended to love the barons but who hated and feared them, had the idea of securing the alienation of their lands. As a result, as time went on, the villeins who by means of hard work had acquired some capital, bought the castles of the noble peers, who had ruined themselves through their own folly. Little by little all the lands changed masters.

The House of Commons became daily more powerful; the older noble families in time died out; and since in England according to the rigor of the law only peers are noble, there would be no more nobility in that country at all if the kings had not created new lords from time to time, and preserved the order of peers, which they once had been so much afraid of, so as to oppose it to that of the commons, now grown too formidable.

All these new peers who compose the upper house receive from the king their title and nothing more; hardly any of them owns the land whose name he bears. One is Duke of Dorset and hasn't an inch of ground in Dorsetshire. Another is Earl of a village and scarcely knows where the village is situated. They have power in parliament but nowhere else.

You hear no talk in this country of high, middle, and low justice, nor of the right of hunting over the property of a citizen who himself has not the liberty of firing a shot in his own field.

A man is not exempt here from paying certain taxes because he is a nobleman or a priest. All taxes are levied by the House of Commons, which, though second in rank, is first in importance.

It is quite within the power of the lords and bishops to reject a tax bill presented by the Commons, but they are not permitted to alter it in any way; they must either pass it or throw it out altogether and without reserve. When a bill is confirmed by the Lords and approved by the king, then everyone pays, each giving not according to his rank (which is absurd) but according to his income: there is no *taille* or arbitrary poll tax, but a real tax on lands, all of which were evaluated under the famous King William III and classified accordingly.

The tax rate remains the same as it was, though the revenues from land have gone up, and so nobody is downtrodden and nobody complains. The feet of the peasant are not tortured by wooden shoes, he eats white bread, he is well clothed, and he is not afraid to increase the number of his cattle or to cover his roof with tile, lest his taxes be raised next year. There are many peasants here who own property amounting to some 200,000 francs, and who do not disdain to keep on cultivating the soil that enriched them and on which they live free.

LETTER TEN

ON COMMERCE

Commerce, which has brought wealth to the citizenry of England, has helped to make them free, and freedom has developed commerce in its turn. By means of it the nation has grown great; it is commerce that little by little has strengthened the naval forces that make the English the masters of the seas. At present they have nearly two hundred warships. Posterity may learn with some surprise that a little island with nothing of its own but a bit of lead, tin, fuller's earth, and coarse wool, became, by means of its commerce, powerful enough by 1723 to send three fleets at one time to three different ends of the earth—one to guard Gibraltar, conquered and kept by its arms; another to Portobello to dispossess the King of Spain of the treasures of the Indies; and the third to the Baltic Sea to prevent the Northern Powers from fighting.[1]

When Louis XIV was shaking Italy, and his armies, already in possession of Savoy and Piedmont, were ready to capture Turin, it was up to Prince Eugene to march from the depths of Germany to the aid of the Duke of Savoy. He had no money at all, a thing without which towns are neither taken nor defended. He appealed to some English merchants. In half an hour he had a loan of fifty millions; whereupon he delivered Turin, beat the French, and wrote this little note to those who had loaned him that sum: "Gentlemen, I have received your money, and I flatter myself that I have employed it to your satisfaction."

All this makes an English merchant justly proud, and allows him boldly to compare himself, not without some reason, to a Roman citizen; moreover, the younger brother of a peer of the

[1] The three fleets go back to the days of Queen Anne; the specific event took place in June of 1726. (Lanson.)

realm does not scorn to enter into trade. Lord Townshend, Minister of State, has a brother who is content to be a merchant in the City. When Lord Oxford was governing England, his younger brother was a factor at Aleppo; he did not want to return home, and died there.

This custom, which unfortunately is beginning to go out of fashion, appears monstrous to Germans infatuated with their quarterings. They are unable to imagine how the son of a peer of England could be only a rich and powerful bourgeois, whereas Germany is all Prince: there have been at one time as many as thirty Highnesses of the same name, with nothing to show for it but pride and a coat of arms.

In France anybody who wants to can be a marquis; and whoever arrives in Paris from the remotest part of some province with money to spend and an *ac* or an *ille* at the end of his name, may indulge in such phrases as "a man of my sort," "a man of my rank and quality," and with sovereign eye look down upon a wholesaler. The merchant himself so often hears his profession spoken of disdainfully that he is fool enough to blush. Yet I don't know which is the more useful to a state, a well-powdered lord who knows precisely what time the king gets up in the morning and what time he goes to bed, and who gives himself airs of grandeur while playing the role of slave in a minister's antechamber, or a great merchant who enriches his country, sends orders from his office to Surat and to Cairo, and contributes to the well-being of the world.

LETTER ELEVEN

ON INOCULATION WITH SMALLPOX

In Christian Europe people gently aver that the English are fools and madmen: fools because they give their children smallpox to keep them from having it; madmen because they lightheartedly communicate to these children a disease that is certain and frightful, with a view to preventing an evil that may never befall them. The English, on their side, say, "The other Europeans are cowardly and unnatural: they are cowardly in fearing to hurt their children a little; unnatural in exposing them to the danger of dying some day of small-pox." To help decide who is right on this question, here is the story of that famous practice of inoculation, which outside England people speak of with such horror.

The women of Circassia have from time immemorial had the custom of giving smallpox to their children, when as little as six months old, by making an incision on the arm and inserting in that incision a pustule that they have carefully removed from the body of another child. That pustule has, in the arm into which it has been slipped, the effect of yeast in dough; it ferments there and spreads through the mass of the blood the characteristics with which it is marked. The pustules of the child who has been given this artificial smallpox are used to carry the same disease to others. The circulation of the disease goes on in Circassia almost without pause; and when unfortunately there is no smallpox at all in the country, people are as much troubled as they are in a bad year else-where.

What caused the rise in Circassia of a custom that appears so strange to other peoples was nevertheless something that the whole earth shares with them, and that is mother-love and self-interest.

The Circassians are poor and their daughters are beautiful, so most of their trade is in them; they furnish with beauties the harems of the Sultan, the Sophy of Persia, and such others as are rich enough to buy and maintain this precious merchandise. With the most honest and virtuous intentions, they bring up these girls to take the initiative with the male sex by caressing them, to improvise dances fraught with lust and voluptuousness, and, by all the most sensual artifices, to revive the appetite of the disdainful masters whom they are destined to serve. Every day these poor creatures rehearse their lessons with their mother, as our little girls recite their catechism, without understanding any of it.

Now it often happened that a father and a mother, after having taken great pains to give their children a good education, suddenly found themselves frustrated in their hopes. Smallpox broke out in the family; one daughter died of it, another lost an eye, a third recovered with a big nose; and the poor parents were ruined, all their resources gone. Often, what is more, when there was an actual epidemic of smallpox, commerce was interrupted for several years, causing a notable diminution in the seraglios of Persia and of Turkey.

A commercial nation is always quick to see its interest, and neglects no branch of learning that may prove useful to its trade. The Circassians observed that, out of a thousand persons, hardly one could be found who had had a complete case of smallpox twice; that in fact some people have undergone three or four light attacks, but never two unequivocal and dangerous ones; that, in a word, no one really gets this disease twice in a lifetime. They noticed also that when smallpox is very benign, and when the eruptions have only a fine and delicate skin to break through, no mark is left on the face. From these natural observations they concluded that if an infant of six months or a year old had a mild case of smallpox, it would not die of it, would not be marked, and would be done with that disease for the rest of its life.

And so, to preserve the life and the beauty of their children, what they had to do was give them smallpox early. That is what they did, inserting in the body of a child a pustule from as completely developed and yet mild a case of small-pox as could be found. The experiment could not fail. The Turks, who are sensible people, immediately adopted the custom, and today there is not a Pasha in Constantinople who doesn't give smallpox to his son and his daughter when they are being weaned.

There are some people who maintain that in ancient times the Circassians learned this custom from the Arabs; but we will leave this historical point to be cleared up by some learned Benedictine, who will not fail to compose on the subject several folio volumes along with the documents. All I have to say on the matter is that at the beginning of the reign of George I, Lady Mary Wortley Montagu, one of the wittiest and most strong-minded women in England, being with her husband on his embassy to Constantinople, took the step, without hesitation, of giving smallpox to a child she had borne in that country. It was no use her chaplain telling her that the experiment was not Christian and could only succeed among infidels: Lady Mary's son recovered splendidly. The lady herself, on her return to London, told her story to the Princess of Wales, who is now queen. It must be acknowl-edged that, apart from titles and crowns, this princess was born to encourage all the arts and to do good to mankind; she is a gracious philosopher on a throne. She has never lost either a chance to learn or a chance to put her generosity to work. It is she who, having learned that a daughter of Milton was still living, and living in poverty, sent her at once the present of a considerable sum; it is she who is the protector of that poor Father Courayer; it is she who condescended to mediate be-tween Dr. Clarke and Mr. Leibniz. As soon as she had heard of the inoculation or insertion of smallpox, she had it tested on four criminals who had been condemned to death. Their lives she doubly saved, for not only did she deliver them from the gallows, but, by means of this artificial smallpox she pre-

vented the natural kind, which they would probably otherwise have caught, and perhaps died of, at a more advanced
age.

The princess, assured of the usefulness of her test, had her
own children inoculated. England followed her example, and
since that time at least ten thousand children of good family
owe their lives, in the same way, to the Queen and to Lady
Mary Wortley Montagu, and as many girls are indebted to
them for their beauty.

Out of every hundred persons in the world, at least sixty
get smallpox; of these sixty, twenty die of it in the most
favorable years, and twenty keep unhappy traces of it with
them for ever. That makes a fifth of mankind for certain,
killed or disfigured by this disease. Of all those who are inoculated in Turkey or in England, not a one dies, unless he is
infirm and condemned to death in other respects; no one is
marked with it; no one gets smallpox a second time, so long
as the inoculation was perfect.

Thus it is certain that if some French ambassadress had
brought this secret from Constantinople to Paris, she would
have rendered a service of everlasting benefit to the nation.
The Duc de Villequier, father of the present Duc d'Aumont,
the best set up and healthiest man in France, would not have
died in the flower of his age; the Prince de Soubise, who enjoyed the most radiant health, would not have been carried
off at the age of twenty-five; Monseigneur, the grandfather of
Louis XV, would not have been buried in his fiftieth year;
twenty thousand persons who died in Paris of smallpox in
1723 would still be alive. Well, then, have the French no
liking for life? Don't their women care about their beauty?
Really, we are odd people! Perhaps ten years from now we
may adopt this English custom, if the curates and the doctors
allow us; or who knows but that within three months the
French will take up inoculation for a whim, if the English
lose their taste for it through fickleness.

I find that the Chinese have practiced this custom for a
hundred years; that is a great recommendation, the example

of a country that passes for being the wisest and most civilized
in the universe. It is true that the Chinese go about it in a
different fashion; they make no incision but give smallpox
through the nose, like snuff. This way is pleasanter, but it
comes to the same thing, and serves equally to confirm the
fact that if inoculation had been practiced in France, the lives
of thousands would have been saved.

ON CHANCELLOR BACON

Not long ago, in a company of well-known persons, the worn-out and frivolous old question was discussed as to who was the greatest man: Caesar, Alexander, Tamerlane, Cromwell, etc.

Someone replied that unquestionably it was Isaac Newton. The man was right; for if true greatness consists in having received a powerful genius from Heaven and in having used it to enlighten oneself and others, such a man as Mr. Newton, the like of whom is not seen in ten centuries, is truly the great man; and these politicians and conquerors, in whom no century has been wanting, are as a rule no more than eminent bad men. It is to him who holds sway over men's minds by force of truth, not to those who make slaves by violent means: it is to him who knows the universe, not to those who disfigure it, that we owe our esteem.

Since you have demanded that I speak about the famous men that England has produced, I must begin with the Bacons, Lockes, Newtons, etc. The generals and ministers will come along in their turn.

I should begin with the famous Lord Verulam, known in Europe under the name of Bacon, which was his family name. He was son of a Keeper of the Seals, and was for a long time Chancellor under King James I. Yet in the midst of court intrigues and the business of his high office, which themselves required a whole man, he found time to be a great philosopher, a good historian, and an elegant writer; and what is even more astonishing, he lived in a century in which the art of writing well was hardly known, and sound philosophy even less so. As is the way of the world, he was more highly valued after his death than during his lifetime: his enemies were courtiers in London; his admirers were found throughout Europe.

When Marquis d'Effiat accompanied to England Princess Marie, the daughter of Henry the Great who was to marry the Prince of Wales, that minister went to visit Bacon, who, being then ill in bed, received him with the curtains closed. "You are like the angels," said d'Effiat to him; "we are always hearing about them, we believe them quite superior to men, and we never have the consolation of seeing them."

You know, sir, how Bacon was accused of a crime which is hardly that of a philosopher—of having allowed himself to be corrupted by money. You know how he was sentenced by the House of Lords to pay a fine of about 400,000 livres in our money,[1] and to lose his station as Chancellor and as peer.

Today the English revere his memory to the point that they do not like to admit that he was guilty. If you ask me what I think, in order to answer you I will help myself to a fine thing I heard Lord Bolingbroke say. They were speaking in his presence of the avarice of which the Duke of Marlborough had been accused, and were citing instances for which they appealed to the testimony of Lord Bolingbroke, who, having been his declared enemy, might perhaps with propriety reveal the facts. "He was so great a man," replied Bolingbroke, "that I have forgotten his vices."

I shall confine myself, then, to speaking to you about what has earned Chancellor Bacon the esteem of Europe.

The most unusual and the best of his works is that which is today the least read and the most useless; I have in mind his *Novum scientiarum organum.* This is the scaffolding by which the new philosophy [2] has been built; and when that edifice had been erected at least in part, the scaffolding was no longer of any use.

Chancellor Bacon was not yet familiar with nature, but he knew and pointed out all the paths that lead to her. He had

[1] The fine was 40,000 pounds sterling, equivalent to 1,000,000 French livres.

[2] "Modern science."

early despised what the universities called Philosophy, and he did all that was in his power to prevent these corporations, founded for the perfecting of human reason, from continuing to ruin it with their *quiddities,* their *abhorrence of a vacuum,* their *substantial forms,* and all the impertinent words that ignorance first made respectable, and that a ridiculous mixture with religion had rendered almost sacred.

He is the father of experimental philosophy. It is quite true that some wonderful discoveries had been made before his day. The mariner's compass had been invented; so had printing, engraving, oil painting, looking glasses; the art of restoring, to some extent, the sight of old people by glasses called spectacles; gunpowder, etc. A new world had been sought, found, and conquered. Who would not suppose that these sublime discoveries had been made by the greatest of philosophers, and in ages much more enlightened than our own? Not at all: it was in an age of the most stupid barbarism that these great changes were made on the earth. Chance alone produced almost all these inventions, and it is even very probable that what we call chance played a large part in the discovery of America. At least we have always believed that Christopher Columbus undertook his voyage solely on the faith of a naval captain whom a storm had driven into the latitude of the Caribbean islands.

At any rate, men knew how to go to the ends of the earth, they knew how to destroy towns with an artificial thunderbolt more terrible than the natural one; but they were not acquainted with the circulation of the blood, the weight of air, the laws of motion, the nature of light, the number of our planets, and so on; and a man who upheld a thesis on the categories of Aristotle, on the universal *à parte rei,* or some other such piece of nonsense, was regarded as a prodigy.

The most astonishing and most useful inventions are not those that do the most honor to the human mind.

It is to a mechanical bent, natural to most men, that we owe all the arts; we do not owe them to sound philosophy. The discovery of fire, the art of making bread, of smelting and working metals, of building houses, the invention of the weaver's shuttle, are of an entirely different order of necessity from printing and the mariner's compass; nevertheless, these arts were devised by men who were still savages.

Later on, what prodigious use the Greeks and the Romans made of mechanics! And yet in their day it was believed that the skies were of crystal, and that the stars were little lamps that sometimes fell into the sea; and one of their great philosophers, after much study, found that the heavenly bodies were pebbles that had broken away from the earth.[3]

In a word, nobody before Chancellor Bacon had understood experimental philosophy; and of all the physical experiments that have been made since his time, hardly one was not suggested in his book. Several of them he had made himself. He constructed pneumatic machines of some sort, by means of which he discovered the elasticity of the air; he went all around the discovery of its weight, he even grazed it, but Torricelli it was who seized upon that truth. Shortly afterward, experimental physics suddenly began to be cultivated in almost all parts of Europe at once. It was a hidden treasure of which Bacon had some expectations, and which all the philosophers, encouraged by his promise, labored to unearth.

But what has surprised me most has been to find in explicit terms in his book that novel theory of attraction which Mr. Newton is credited with inventing.

"We must try to discover," says Bacon, "whether there is not some kind of magnetic power which operates between the earth and heavy bodies, between the moon and the ocean, between the planets," etc.

In another place he says:

It must be either that heavy bodies tend by their nature toward the center of the earth or else that they are mutually attracted by it; and, in this latter case, it is evident that the closer falling bodies approach to the earth, the more forcibly they are drawn to it.

3 Voltaire, like a good modern, does less than justice to ancient science.

He continues:

> We ought to find by experiment whether the same clock
> moved by weights will go faster on the top of a mountain
> or at the bottom of a mine. If the force of the weights
> diminishes on the mountain and increases in the mine, then
> it is likely that the earth has a real power of attraction.[4]

This precursor in philosophy was also an elegant writer, a
historian, a wit.

His moral essays are highly regarded, but they were written
to instruct rather than to please; and being neither a satire on
human nature like the maxims of M. de La Rochefoucauld,
nor a school for skepticism like Montaigne, they are less read
than these two ingenious books.

His *History of Henry VII* has been considered a masterpiece; but I should be much mistaken if it deserved to be
compared with the work of our excellent de Thou.

Discussing that famous impostor Perkin, a Jew by birth,
who, encouraged by the Duchess of Burgundy, so boldly took
the name of Richard IV, King of England, and disputed the
crown with Henry VII, here is how Chancellor Bacon expresses himself:

> At this time the King began again to be haunted with
> sprites; by the magic and curious arts of the Lady Margaret;
> who raised up the ghost of Richard Duke of York . . . to
> walk and vex the King. . . .
> After such time as she thought he [Perkin] was perfect in
> his lesson, she began to cast with herself from what coast
> this blazing star should first appear, and at what time. It
> must be upon the horizon of Ireland; for there had the like
> meteor strong influence before." [5]

4 Voltaire has freely pieced together the original. For the first passage,
see *Novum Organum*, II, xlv; for the second, II, xxxvi.

5 *The Works of Francis Bacon*, ed. Spedding, Ellis, and Heath (London,
1878), Vol. VI, pp. 132, 135. In his translation Voltaire found himself able
to omit the last clause. (Also his eye picked up Edward IV in mistake
for the son Richard.)

Environ ce temps, le roi Henri fut obsédé d'esprits malins par la
magie de la duchesse de Bourgogne, qui évoqua des enfers l'ombre

It seems to me that our sensible de Thou does not indulge in this fustian, which in the old days was taken for the sublime, but which we now rightly call galimatias.

---

d'Édouard IV pour venir tourmenter le roi Henri. Quand la duchesse de Bourgogne eut instruit Parkins [sic], elle commença à délibérer par quelle région du Ciel elle ferait paraître cette comète, et elle résolut qu'elle éclaterait d'abord sur l'horizon de l'Irlande.

LETTER THIRTEEN

ON MR. LOCKE

Perhaps there has never been a wiser, more orderly mind, or a logician more exact, than Mr. Locke; and yet he was no great mathematician. He never could submit to the drudgery of calculations, nor to the dryness of mathematical truths, which in themselves offer nothing concrete to the understanding; at the same time no one has better demonstrated than he that one may have a geometrical intellect without the help of geometry. Great philosophers before his time had positively determined what the soul of man is; but since they knew absolutely nothing about the matter, it is quite proper that they should all have been of different opinions.

In Greece, the cradle of arts and errors, where the grandeur and foolishness of the human mind were carried so far, people reasoned about the soul as we do.

The Divine Anaxagoras, to whom an altar was raised for teaching mankind that the sun is larger than the Peloponnesus, that snow is black, and that the heavens are made of stone, declared that the soul is an airy spirit but nevertheless immortal.

Diogenes—another than the one who became a cynic after having been a counterfeiter—asserted that the soul is a portion of the very substance of God, and that idea at least was a brilliant one.

Epicurus saw it as composed of parts, like the body; Aristotle, who has been explicated in a thousand ways because he was unintelligible, believed—if we can trust some of his disciples—that the human understanding is a single universal substance.

The divine Plato, master of the divine Aristotle; and the divine Socrates, master of the divine Plato, called the soul corporeal and eternal. No doubt the *daimon* of Socrates had

told him all about it. It is true there are people who maintain
that a man who bragged of having a familiar spirit was without question either a madman or a knave, but such people
are too hard to please.

As for our Fathers of the Church, several of them in the
earlier centuries believed the human soul, the angels, and God
himself to be corporeal.

The world is getting subtler every day. St. Bernard, as
Father Mabillon admits, taught that after death the soul did
not see God in heaven but conversed only with the humanity
of Jesus Christ. This time they did not take his word for it;
the adventure of the Crusade had somewhat discredited his
oracles. A thousand scholastic philosophers came after him,
such as the Irrefragable Doctor, the Subtle Doctor, the Angelic
Doctor, the Seraphic Doctor, the Cherubic Doctor,[1] all of
whom have been quite sure they knew the soul through and
through, but have never failed to discuss the subject as if they
wanted nobody to understand a word of it.

Our Descartes, born to bring to light the errors of antiquity
and to put his own in their place, being led astray by that
spirit of system which blinds the greatest of men, imagined
he had demonstrated that soul is the same thing as thought,
just as matter, according to him, is the same as extension. He
maintained that we are perpetually thinking, and that the
soul makes its arrival in the body already provided with every
possible metaphysical notion, knowing God, space, and infinity, as well as the whole range of abstract ideas, and filled,
in other words, with splendid knowledge all of which it unfortunately forgets as it leaves its mother's womb.

M. Malebranche, of the Oratory, in his sublime hallucina-
tions, not only allowed the existence of innate ideas but was
certain that all we perceive is in God and that God, so to
speak, is our soul.

After so many deep thinkers had fashioned the romance of
the soul, there came a wise man who modestly recounted its

[1] Alexander Hales, John Duns Scotus, St. Thomas Aquinas, St. Bonaventura, and, fifth, a joke borrowed from Rabelais.

true history: Locke has unfolded to man the nature of human reason as a fine anatomist explains the powers of the body. Throughout his work he makes use of the torch of science. He dares sometimes to affirm, but he also dares to doubt. Instead of defining at once what we know nothing about, he examines, bit by bit, that which we want to understand. He takes a child at the moment of birth, he follows step by step the growth of its understanding, he marks what it has in common with animals, and in what ways it is superior to them. Above all, he consults his own experience, the consciousness of his own thought.

> But whether (he says) the soul be supposed to exist antecedent to, or coeval with, or some time after the first rudiments of organization, or the beginnings of life in the body, I leave to be disputed by those who have better thought of that matter. I confess myself to have one of those dull souls, that doth not perceive itself always to contemplate ideas; nor can conceive it any more necessary for the soul always to think, than for the body always to move. . . .[2]

As for me, I am proud of the honor of being in this respect as stupid as Locke, for no one will ever convince me that I am always thinking. And I am no more disposed than he is to imagine that a few weeks after my conception I was an exceedingly learned soul, knowing a thousand things that I later forgot in being born, having quite fruitlessly arrived *in utero* at mental attainments that were swept away as soon as I could have any use for them, and that I have never since been able to recover.

[2] *Essay Concerning Human Understanding*, Book II, Chapter I, Section 10. Voltaire's version of this passage, drawn from the translation of Coste, is free yet not misleading.

"Je laisse, dit-il, à discuter à ceux qui en savent plus que moi, si notre âme existe avant ou après l'organisation de notre corps; mais j'avoue qu'il m'est tombé en partage une de ces âmes grossières qui ne pensent pas toujours, et j'ai même le malheur de ne pas concevoir qu'il soit plus nécessaire à l'âme de penser toujours qu'au corps d'être toujours en mouvement."

Having done away with innate ideas, having altogether renounced the vanity of believing that we are always thinking,
Locke proves that all our ideas come to us through the senses,
examines our ideas both simple and complex, follows the
human mind in all its operations, and shows the imperfections
of all the languages spoken by man, and our constant abuse
of terms. He comes at last to consider the extent, or rather
the nothingness, of human knowledge. It is in this chapter
that he humbly ventures to suggest that "possibly we shall
never be able to know whether any mere material being thinks
or no." [3] These sage words struck more than one theologian
as a scandalous declaration that the soul is material and
mortal.

Certain Englishmen, pious in their way, gave the alarm.
The superstitious are in society what cowards are in an army:
they are seized by, and they spread, panic terror. The cry went
up that Locke was trying to overturn religion.[4] This was not
a religious matter, though; it was a purely philosophic one,
quite independent of faith and of revelation. All people had
to do was to consider without bitterness whether there is any
contradiction in saying, "Matter can think," and whether or
not God is able to infuse thought into matter. But theologians
have a bad habit of complaining that God is outraged when
someone has simply failed to be of their opinion. They are too
much like the bad poets who, because Boileau was making
fun of them, accused him of speaking offensively of the King.

Doctor Stillingfleet [5] acquired the reputation of a moderate
theologian by not saying anything positively abusive to Locke.
He entered the lists against him but was beaten; for he

[3] Book IV, Chapter III, Section 6. For "any mere material being"
Locke had first written "matter."

[4] See, for instance, Thomas Burnet, *Remarks upon an Essay Concerning Humane Understanding* (London, 1697-99); Henry Lee, *Antisceptic-
ism, or Notes upon Each Chapter of Locke's Essay* (London, 1702).

[5] Edward Stillingfleet (1635-99), Bishop of Worcester, published three
pamphlets (1696-97) in a controversy with Locke on the doctrine of the
Trinity.

argued as a man of learning, and Locke as a philosopher who was acquainted with the strength and weakness of the human mind and fought with weapons whose temper he knew.

If I were so bold as to speak after Mr. Locke on so ticklish a subject, I should say: Men have been wrangling for a long time over the nature and immortality of the soul. As for its immortality, that is impossible to prove since we are still arguing over its nature, and since, in order to determine whether something that exists is immortal or not, we surely must first be thoroughly familiar with it. The human reason is so little capable of proving by its own means the immortality of the soul that religion has been obliged to reveal it to us. The common good of mankind requires that we believe the soul immortal; faith commands it; nothing more is necessary, and the question is settled. The nature of the soul is a different matter; religion cares little what the soul is made of so long as it is virtuous. It is a clock we have been given to regulate; but the craftsman who made it has not told us the composition of the spring.

I am a body, and I think; that is all I know. Shall I go and attribute to an unknown cause what I can so easily attribute to the only secondary cause I know? Here all the philosophers of the School [6] interrupt and say, "The body has only extension and solidity, and it is capable only of movement and of figure.[7] Now movement, figure, extension, and solidity cannot produce an idea, and thus the soul cannot be material." This great piece of reasoning, which has been so often repeated, may be reduced to these words:

I am totally ignorant of the nature of matter; I make imperfect conjectures as to some of its properties. Now I am

---

[6] Cartesian. Voltaire, the reader may have guessed, admired "Our Descartes who was the greatest philosopher in Europe, before Sir Isaac Newton appeared . . ." (Dedication of *La Henriade* to the Queen of England, 1728), and wished that Descartes had more often followed his own Method, as laid down, for instance, in the first precept, "never to accept anything as true unless I know it certainly to be so."

[7] Shape, form, objectively describable bounds.

totally ignorant as to whether there is any possible connection between these properties and idea or thought. Thus, because I know nothing whatsoever, I positively affirm that matter is incapable of thought.

There, plainly, is the School's way of reasoning. Locke would say to these gentlemen with perfect simplicity, "Confess at least that you know as little as I. Your imagination no more than mine can conceive how it is that a body should have ideas; do you understand any better how any substance whatever should have them? You comprehend neither matter nor spirit; how then do you dare affirm anything?"

Then, in his turn, comes the superstitious man, and he says that those who suspect that thought is possible with the sole aid of the body ought to be burnt for the good of their souls. But what would such people say if it were they themselves that were guilty of irreligion? In fact, what man could venture to assert, without an absurd impiety, that it is impossible for the Creator to give thought and feeling to matter! See now, if you please, to what straits you are reduced, you who thus limit the power of the Creator! The animals have the same organs as we, the same feelings, the same perceptions; they have a memory, they combine certain ideas. If God has been unable to animate matter and to give it feeling, then one of two things is true: either animals are mere machines, or else they have a soul.

It appears to me almost certain that animals cannot be mere machines. Here is my proof: God made for them precisely the same sense organs as our own, and so if they do not feel, God has made a useless work. Now even you acknowledge that God does nothing in vain, and so He has not manufactured all those organs of feeling in order that no feeling should be done with them, and therefore animals are not mere machines.

Since according to you the animals cannot have a soul, there is, like it or not, nothing for you to say but that God gave to the organs of animals, which are matter, the faculty of feeling and perceiving, which in them you call instinct.

Well now, who can prevent God from imparting to our more subtle organs that faculty of feeling, perceiving, and thinking which we call human reason? Wherever you turn you are obliged to confess your ignorance and the boundless power of the Creator; cease then to struggle against the wise and unassuming philosophy of Locke. Far from being opposed to religion, it would serve as proof if religion had need of it. For what philosophy is more religious than that which, affirming only what it clearly understands, and able to own to its weakness, tells us that no sooner do we examine first principles than we must have recourse to God.

Besides, we should never fear that any philosophical opinion could harm the religion of a country. Let our Mysteries be contrary to our demonstrations, they are no less revered for it by Christian philosophers, who know that matters of reason and matters of faith are different in nature. Never will philosophers set up a religious sect. Why? Because they do not write for the people, and because they are without enthusiasm.[8]

Divide the human race into twenty parts. Nineteen of them are composed of those who work with their hands, and will never know if there is a Locke in the world or not. In the remaining twentieth part how few men do we find who read! And among those who do read there are twenty who read novels for every one who studies philosophy. The number of those who think is exceedingly small, and they are not aiming to disturb the world.

It is not Montaigne, nor Locke, nor Bayle, nor Spinoza, nor Hobbes, nor Lord Shaftesbury, nor Mr. Collins, nor Mr. Toland, and so on, who have carried the torch of discord in their native country; it is theologians, for the most part, who having first had the ambition of being leaders of their sect,

8 Voltaire, in following Locke, is using the word "enthusiasm" in the then popular sense of "Fancied inspiration; 'a vain confidence of divine favour or communication,'" if not of "Ill-regulated or misdirected religious emotion, extravagance of religious speculation." (O.E.D.)

have soon afterward desired to be heads of parties. Why, all the books of the modern philosophers put together will never make as much noise in the world as once was made just by the dispute of the Cordeliers [9] over the shape of their sleeve and their hood.

[9] Greyfriars, Franciscans.

LETTER FOURTEEN

ON DESCARTES AND NEWTON

A Frenchman arriving in London finds quite a change, in philosophy as in all else. Behind him he left the world full; here he finds it empty. In Paris one sees the universe composed of vortices of subtle matter; in London one sees nothing of the sort. With us, it's the pressure of the moon that causes the rising of the tide; with the English, it's the sea gravitating toward the moon; so that when you think the moon ought to give us high tide, these gentlemen think it ought to be low; none of which unfortunately can be verified, for in order to know the truth of it we should have had to examine the moon and the tides at the first moment of creation.

You will also notice that the sun, which in France has nothing to do with the business, over here contributes his twenty-five per cent or so. According to your Cartesians, everything is done by means of an impulse that is practically incomprehensible; according to Mr. Newton it is by a kind of attraction, the reason for which is no better known. In Paris you picture the earth as shaped like a melon; in London it is flattened on both sides. Light, for a Cartesian, exists in the air; for a Newtonian it comes here from the sun in six and a half minutes. All the operations of your chemistry are owing to acids, alkalis, and subtle matter; in England, the concept of attraction dominates even in this.

The very essence of things is totally different. You agree neither on the definition of soul nor on that of matter. Descartes assures us that soul is the same thing as thought, and Locke pretty well demonstrates the contrary.

Descartes declares, again, that matter is nothing but extension; to that, Newton adds solidity. Here are some tremendous contrarieties.

Non nostrum inter vos tantas componere lites.[1]

This famous Newton, this destroyer of the Cartesian system, died in March of last year, 1727. In life he was honored by his countrymen, and he was buried like a king who had benefited his subjects.

The eulogy on Mr. Newton that was delivered by M. de Fontenelle before the Académie des Sciences has been read with eagerness, and has been translated into English. In England people looked forward to the opinion of M. de Fontenelle, expecting a solemn declaration of the superiority of English philosophy, but when they found him comparing Descartes to Newton, the whole Royal Society of London was aroused. Far from acquiescing in such a judgment, they found a good deal of fault with the discourse. Several even (and those by no means the most philosophical) were shocked at the comparison for the sole reason that Descartes was a Frenchman.

It must be confessed that these two great men were remarkably unlike in their way of life, in their fortune, and in their philosophy.

Descartes was born with a lively and strong imagination which made of him a man as extraordinary in his private life as in his thinking. That imagination could not be concealed even in his philosophical works, where at every moment one is struck by ingenious and sparkling comparisons. Nature had almost made him a poet, and as a matter of fact he did compose for the Queen of Sweden an entertainment in verse which, for the honor of his memory, has not been printed.

He tried the profession of arms for a while, and afterward, having become a philosopher altogether, thought it not unworthy of himself to have a love affair. He had by his mistress a daughter named Francine, who died young, and whose loss he deeply mourned. And so he experienced all that belongs to the human lot.

[1] "It is not for me to settle such high debate as that between you."— Virgil, Eclogues, III, 108.

For a long time he believed that in order to philosophize freely he would have to escape from society, and especially from his native country. He was right; the men of his time knew too little to help him clarify his ideas, and were in fact capable of little more than doing him harm.

He left France because he followed after truth, which was persecuted there in those days by the miserable philosophy of scholasticism; but he found no more rationality in the universities of Holland, to which he retired. For while the sole propositions of his philosophy that were true were condemned in France, he was also persecuted by the pretended philosophers of Holland, who understood him no better, and who, having a nearer view of his glory, hated him personally even more. He was obliged to leave Utrecht. He had to undergo the accusation of atheism, the last resource of calumniators; he who had employed all his intellectual sagacity in a search for new proofs of the existence of a God was suspected of believing in none.

Such a deal of persecution presumes very great merit and a brilliant reputation; both were his. Reason even began to gleam a little in the world, piercing through the darkness of scholasticism and the prejudices of popular superstition. At last his name became so famous that there was some effort to attract him to France with the promise of rewards. A pension of a thousand *écus* was offered him. He came back with that expectation, paid the expenses of the patent (which was sold in those days), failed to receive the pension, and returned to philosophize in his North Holland solitude at the same time as the great Galileo, at the age of eighty, groaned in the prisons of the Inquisition for having proved the motion of the earth. In the end he died in Stockholm, prematurely, of a bad regimen, in the presence of a number of learned men, his enemies, and in the hands of a physician who loathed him.

The career of Sir Isaac Newton was altogether different. He lived for eighty-five years, always tranquil and happy, and held in honor in his own country. It was his great good fortune to have been born not only in a free country but in a time when, the irrelevancies of scholasticism being banished, reason alone was cultivated; and the world must needs be his pupil, not his enemy.

One curious difference between him and Descartes is that in the course of so long a life he was free from both passion and weakness. He never had intimacies with a woman; this was confirmed to me by the doctor and the surgeon in whose arms he died. One may admire Newton for it, but one should not blame Descartes.

According to public opinion in England, of these two philosophers the first was a dreamer and the other a sage.

Few people in London read Descartes, whose works, in effect, have lost their utility; hardly any read Newton either, for it takes considerable knowledge to understand him. Nevertheless, everybody talks about them, granting nothing to the Frenchman and everything to the Englishman. Some folk believe that if we are no longer satisfied with the abhorrence of vacuums, if we know that air has weight, if we use telescopes, we owe it all to Newton. Over here he is the Hercules of fable, to whom the ignorant attributed all the deeds of the other heroes.

In a criticism made in London of M. Fontenelle's discourse, somebody went so far as to say that Descartes was not a great geometrician. Those who talk in this way may reproach themselves for beating their nurse. Descartes made as great progress, from the point at which he found geometry to the point to which he carried it, as Newton did after him. He was the first who found the way to give the algebraic equations of curves. His geometry, which thanks to him has by now become a commonplace, was in his time so profound that no professor dared undertake to explain it, and no one in Holland understood it but Schooten, and no one in France but Fermat.

He carried the same spirit of geometry and inventiveness over into dioptrics, which in his hands became a new art entirely; and if here or there he made a mistake, it is clear that a man who discovers new lands cannot suddenly know all there is to know about them. Those who come after him and make those lands bear fruit at least owe their discovery to him. I will not deny that all the other works of M. Descartes swarm with errors.

Geometry was a guide that, in a way, he himself had created and that would have conducted him safely through physics; he abandoned that guide in the end, however, and gave himself up to the systematizing spirit. From then on, his philosophy was no more than an ingenious romance,[2] at best seeming probable to the ignorant. He erred on the nature of the soul, on the proofs of the existence of God, on the subject of matter, on the laws of motion, on the nature of light. He admitted innate ideas, he invented new elements, he created a world, he made man according to his own fashion—in fact, it is rightly said that man according to Descartes is Descartes' man, far removed from man as he actually is.

He carried his errors in metaphysics so far as to assert that two and two make four only because God has willed it so. But it is not too much to say that he was admirable even in his aberrations. When he was wrong, at least he was systematically wrong, and with logical coherence. He got rid of the absurd chimeras with which we had infatuated our youth for two thousand years. He taught the men of his time how to reason, and how to fight him with his own weapons. If he has not paid in sterling, it is certainly something to have decried the counterfeit.

I do not think one can truly compare his philosophy in any way with that of Newton: the first is an experimental sketch, the second a finished masterpiece. But he who has set us on the road to truth is perhaps as worthy as he who since then has gone on to the end of it.

Descartes gave sight to the blind; they saw the faults of antiquity and their own as well. The course he opened to us

[2] (See Letter IV, note 1.) Roger Cotes, in his preface (1713) to the second edition of Newton's *Principia*, uses this phrase to describe the work of philosophers who build accurately on hypotheses. James Thomson, in the unrevised "To the Memory of Sir Isaac Newton," as first published in folio, June, 1727, had referred to Descartes as "the French dreamer."

has since become boundless. The little book of Rohaut [3] offered us for a while a complete system of physics; today, the collected works of all the academies of Europe do not amount even to the beginnings of a system. On going deep down into that abyss, we found it infinite.

Now we shall see what Mr. Newton dug out of it.

[3] *Traité de physique* (1671), republished as late as 1730.

ON THE SYSTEM OF ATTRACTION

The discoveries of Sir Isaac Newton,[1] which have brought him such universal fame, have to do with the system of the world, with light, with infinity in geometry, and last with chronology, which he played with for relaxation.

I will tell you (without verbiage, if I can) the little that I have been able to get hold of among all these sublime ideas.

As for the system of our world: there had long been dispute over what it is that causes all the planets to revolve, and what keeps them in their orbits, and also over what causes all bodies here below to come down to the surface of the earth.

The system of Descartes, expounded and much altered since his time, gave a plausible reason for these phenomena, and that reason appeared all the more true for being simple and intelligible to everybody. But in philosophy we must beware of what we think we understand too easily, as well as of what we do not understand at all.

Gravity, the increase of speed in bodies falling to earth, the revolution of the planets in their orbits, their rotation around their axes—all that is nothing but motion. Now motion cannot be conceived except by impulsion; hence all bodies are impelled. But by what? All space is full; then it is filled with a very subtle matter, for we do not perceive it; then this matter goes from west to east, since it is from west to east that all the planets are impelled. So, from conjecture to conjecture, and from probability to probability, there grew in the mind a vast vortex of subtle matter in which the planets are whirled

[1] In writing on Newton, Voltaire leaned heavily on Henry Pemberton's *A View of Sir Isaac Newton's Philosophy* (1728), on Fontenelle's *Éloge de Newton*, on the *Discours sur les différentes figures des astres* (1732) by Maupertuis, and on his correspondence with the latter.

around the sun. In addition an individual vortex is created, floating in the great one and turning daily around the planet. When all that is done, we assert that gravity is the result of this daily movement; for, we say, the subtile matter which turns about our little vortex must go seventeen times as fast as the earth; now if it goes seventeen times as fast as the earth, it must exert immensely more centrifugal force and, consequently, thrust all bodies toward the earth. And that is the cause of gravity according to the Cartesian system.

But before calculating the centrifugal force and speed of this subtile matter, they ought to have made sure that it exists at all; and supposing that it does, still the possibility of its being the cause of gravity has been shown to be false.

Mr. Newton seems utterly to annihilate all these vortices, great and small, the one that carries the planets about the sun as well as that which makes each planet turn on its own axis.

First, with regard to the supposed small vortex of the earth, it is established that little by little it must lose its motion; it is established that if the earth floats in a fluid, that fluid must be of the same density as the earth, and if that fluid is of the same density, all bodies that we move must encounter tremendous resistance—that is to say that to raise a pound's weight you would need a lever as long as the earth.

Secondly, as for great vortices, they are even more fantastic. It is impossible to reconcile them with the laws of Kepler, the truth of which has been proved. Mr. Newton shows that the revolution of the fluid in which Jupiter is supposedly rolled along is not to the revolution of the fluid of the earth as the revolution of Jupiter is to that of the earth.

He proves that, since all the planets revolve in ellipses, and consequently are much farther from one another at their aphelions and much nearer at their perihelions, the earth, for example, ought to go faster when it is nearer Venus and Mars, since the fluid that carries it along, being then under more pressure, must move faster; and yet it is just then that the motion of the earth is slower.

He proves that there is no such thing as a celestial matter that travels from west to east, since comets traverse these spaces sometimes from east to west, sometimes from north to south.

Finally, to settle the question more thoroughly if possible, he proves or at least shows it to be most likely (by means of experiments even) that the Plenum is impossible, and so he restores to us the Void, which Aristotle and Descartes had banished from the world.

Since, with these arguments and many others as well, he had upset the vortices of Cartesianism, he despaired of ever being in a position to know whether there is a secret principle in nature that is the cause of the movements of all the heavenly bodies and that also makes for gravity on the earth. Having withdrawn in 1666 into the country near Cambridge, one day as he walked in his garden and noticed fruit falling from a tree he drifted off into deep meditation on that problem of gravity, of which all the philosophers have so long vainly sought the cause, and in which the vulgar find nothing the slightest bit mysterious. He said to himself, "From whatever height in our hemisphere these bodies should fall, their descent would certainly be in the progression discovered by Galileo, and the distances covered by them would be as the squares of the times. This power that causes heavy bodies to go downward is the same, without any noticeable diminution, at whatever depth one may be within the earth and on the highest mountain. Why should this power not extend so far as the moon? And if it is true that it carries so far, is there not a great likelihood that this power holds it in its orbit and determines its movement? But if the moon does obey this power, whatever it may be, isn't it again very reasonable to suppose that the other planets are equally subject to it?

"If this power exists, it ought to increase (which has moreover been proved) inversely as the squares of the distances. All that remains is to compare the distance covered by a heavy body in falling to earth from a moderate height, with the distance covered in the same length of time by a body falling from the orbit of the moon. To learn what we wish to know, we only need the measurements of the earth and the distance to it from the moon."

That is how Mr. Newton reasoned it out. But in England at the time the only measurements of the globe were very faulty ones; it was all left to the uncertain estimates of pilots, who reckoned sixty English miles to a degree of latitude, whereas they should have reckoned nearly seventy. Since this inaccurate calculation did not agree with the conclusions that Mr. Newton wished to draw, he abandoned them. A mediocre philosopher, one filled only with vanity, would have squared the measure of the earth with his own system as well as he could. Mr. Newton preferred at the time to abandon his project. But after M. Picart had measured the earth exactly, in tracing that Meridian which does so much honor to France, Mr. Newton resumed his first ideas and found what he wanted with the calculations of M. Picart. It has always seemed extraordinary to me that such sublime verities should have been discovered with the aid of a quadrant and a little arithmetic.

The circumference of the earth is one hundred twenty-three million two hundred forty-nine thousand six hundred Paris feet.[2] From that alone may be derived the whole system of *attraction*.

We know the circumference of the earth, we know that of the moon's orbit, and the diameter of that orbit. The revolution of the moon in that orbit is completed in twenty-seven days, seven hours, forty-three minutes. Thus it is clear that the moon averages one hundred eighty-seven thousand nine hundred and sixty Paris feet a minute; and, by a familiar theorem, it is demonstrated that the central force which would make a body fall from the height of the moon would bring it down only fifteen Paris feet in the first minute.

Now, if the law by which bodies bear down, gravitate, are attracted in an inverse ratio to the squares of the distances is true; if it is the same power that acts according to this law

2 Newton: *"pedum Parisiensium."* The French foot was .078 inches longer than the English one.

throughout nature; it is evident that, the earth being sixty radii distant from the moon, a heavy body must fall to earth fifteen feet in the first second, and fifty-four thousand feet in the first minute.

It is a fact that a heavy body falls fifteen feet in the first second, and during the first minute covers fifty-four thousand feet, which figure is the square of sixty multiplied by fifteen; therefore, heavy bodies gravitate in an inverse ratio to the squares of the distances; therefore, the same power makes for gravity on the earth and holds the moon in its orbit.

Once it is demonstrated that the moon gravitates to the earth, which is the center of its particular motion, it is demonstrated that the earth and the moon gravitate to the sun, which is the center of their annual motion.

The other planets must equally be subject to this general law, and, if this law obtains, these planets must follow the laws discovered by Kepler. All these laws, all these relationships are in fact observed by the planets with the greatest exactitude; hence the power of gravitation pulls all the planets, like our own globe, toward the sun. Finally, since the reaction of every body is proportional to the action exerted upon it, we may be certain that the earth in its turn gravitates to the moon, and that the sun gravitates to both one and the other; that each of the satellites of Saturn gravitates to the other four and the other four to it, all five to Saturn, and Saturn to all five; that it is the same with Jupiter, and that all these globes are attracted by the sun, and the sun in turn by them.

This force of gravitation is exerted in proportion to the quantity of matter a body contains—a truth that Mr. Newton proved by experiment. This new discovery has served to show that the sun, the center of all the planets, attracts them all in direct proportion to their mass, combined with their distance. From there, rising by degrees to a kind of knowledge that seemed not to have been made for the human mind, he boldly calculates how much matter the sun contains, and how much is to be found in each planet; and thus he shows that, according to the simple laws of mechanics, every celestial

globe must necessarily be just where it is. His principle of
the laws of gravitation alone explains all the apparent irregularities in the motion of the heavenly bodies. The inequalities
of the moon's motion follow necessarily from these laws. In
addition, it becomes perfectly clear why the nodes of the
moon's orbit complete their revolution in nineteen years, and
those of the earth in about twenty-six thousand. The flux and
reflux of the sea is another very simple result of attraction.
The nearness of the moon when full and when new, and its
remoteness at the quarters, combined with the influence of
the sun, obviously explain the rise and fall of the ocean.

Once he had by means of his sublime theory accounted for
the motion and inequalities of the planets, he bridled the
comets with the same law. These beacons, so long a mystery,
which have terrified the world and shipwrecked philosophy,
which were by Aristotle situated below the moon, and by
Descartes ordered to stand above Saturn, have at last been put
in their right place by Newton.

He proves that they are solid bodies, which move within
the sphere of action of the sun, and describe an ellipse so eccentric and so nearly a parabola that certain comets take more
than five hundred years to complete their course.

Mr. Halley believes that the comet of 1680 is the same as
appeared in the time of Julius Caesar. That one is more useful than others in showing that comets are hard and opaque
bodies. For it came so close to the sun as to be only a sixth
of its diameter away from it; consequently, it had to rise to
a degree of heat two thousand times greater than that of the
fieriest iron. It would have been dissolved and consumed very
shortly if it had not been an opaque body.

The fashion of foretelling the courses of comets was then
beginning. The celebrated mathematician, Jacques Bernoulli,
following his own system, concluded that the famous comet
of 1680 would reappear on the 17th of May, 1719. Not an
astronomer in Europe went to bed on that night of the 17th
of May, but the famous comet failed to appear. There is at
least more adroitness, if not more certainty, in giving it five

hundred and seventy-five years to turn up again. An English geometrician named Wilston, no less fanciful than mathematical, seriously asserted that at the time of the Deluge there had been a comet, which he held responsible for the inundation of our globe; and he was so unjust as to be astonished when people laughed at him. The ancient world thought in much the same way as Wilston; it believed that comets were always the harbingers of some great earthly disaster. Newton, on the contrary, suspects that they all are most beneficent, and that their exhalations only serve to relieve and quicken the planets, which, in their courses, drink up all the particles that have been detached from comets by the sun. This sentiment is at least more probable than the other.

That is not all. If this force of gravitation, of attraction, is at work in all the celestial globes, it doubtless acts on all parts of those globes; for if bodies attract one another in proportion to their masses, it can only be in proportion to the quantity of their parts; and if this force resides in the whole, it certainly resides in the half, in the quarter, in the eighth part, and so on to infinity. In addition, if this power were not distributed equally in every part, there would always be some parts of the globe that would gravitate more than the others —which does not happen. Therefore this force really exists in all matter, and in the smallest particles of it.

So there is *attraction,* the great means by which all nature is moved.

Newton had rightly foreseen, after having demonstrated the reality of this principle, that there would be resistance to the mere name of it. In more than one place in his book he cautions his reader about attraction itself, warning him not to confuse it with the occult qualities of the ancients, and to content themselves with the knowledge that in all bodies there is a central force which, from one end of the universe to the other, acts on the nearest bodies and on the most remote, according to the immutable laws of mechanics.

It is surprising that after the solemn protestations of this great philosopher, M. Saurin and M. de Fontenelle, who themselves deserve the name, should have reproached him explicitly for holding to the absurdities of Peripateticism: M. Saurin in the Memoirs of the Academy of 1709, and M. de Fontenelle in his very eulogy of Mr. Newton.

Almost all the French, whether learned or not, have repeated this reproach. Everywhere one hears them say: "Why didn't Newton use the word *impulsion,* which people understand so well, rather than *attraction,* which they don't understand at all?"

Newton could have replied to his critics: "In the first place, you don't understand the word *impulsion* any better than you do the word *attraction,* and if you cannot conceive how it is that one body is drawn toward the center of another, neither can you imagine by what means a body can push at that of another.

"Secondly, I have been unable to admit *impulsion;* for in order to do so I should have had to know that the planets are actually pushed by some sort of celestial matter; whereas, not only am I not acquainted with any such matter, I have proved that it does not exist.

"Thirdly, I use the word *attraction* only to express an effect that I have discovered in nature: the certain and indisputable effect of an unknown principle, a quality inherent in matter, of which cleverer men than I will find the cause, if they can."

"What have you taught us, then," they go on doggedly, "and why all that figuring in order at last to inform us about something you yourself do not understand?"

"I have taught you," Newton might reply, "that the mechanics of central forces makes all bodies gravitate in proportion to the matter they contain, and that these central forces alone cause the planets and comets to move in marked proportion. I have demonstrated that it is impossible there should be another cause of gravity and of the movement of all the heavenly bodies; for with heavy bodies falling to earth according to the proved proportion of central forces, and the planets completing their courses following these same proportions, if there were yet another power acting on all these bodies it would increase their speeds or alter their directions. Now not one of these bodies ever shows a single degree of motion, of speed, of determination, which has not been demonstrated to be the effect of central forces. Thus it is impossible that there should be another power."

Permit me to give you another moment of Newton talking. Will he not be welcome when he says: "My position is very different from that of the ancients. They saw, for example, water rise in pumps, and they said, 'The water rises because it abhors a vacuum.' But I am in the position of the first person who ever noticed that water rises in pumps, and who left it to others to explain the cause of that effect. The first anatomist to say that the arm moves because the muscles contract, taught mankind an incontestable truth; do we owe him any the less for his not having known why the muscles contract? The cause of the elasticity of air is unknown, but the man who discovered this elasticity did a great service to the study of physics. Since the force that I have discovered was both more hidden and more universal, I ought to get all the more thanks. I have discovered a new property of matter, one of the Creator's secrets; I have calculated, I have demonstrated its effects; can they now cavil with me over the name I give it?

"It is vortices that can be called an occult quality, since their existence has never been proved. Attraction, on the contrary, is a reality, since its effects are demonstrated, and proportions calculated. The cause of that cause is in the bosom of God."

Procedes huc, et non ibis amplius.[3]

3 Should be *"Usque huc venies, et non procedes amplius"*: "Hitherto shalt thou come, but no further."—Job 38:11.

ON NEWTON'S OPTICS

A new universe was discovered by the philosophers of the last century, one that was all the more difficult to understand as people did not even suspect that it existed. The wisest felt that there was some temerity in so much as dreaming that one could divine the laws by which the heavenly bodies move and by which light manifests itself.

Galileo, through his astronomical discoveries; Kepler, by means of his calculations; Descartes, at least in his dioptrics; and Newton in all his works, saw into the mechanics of the forces at work in the world. In geometry the infinite was subjected to calculation. The circulation of the blood in animals and of sap in plants changed our view of nature. In the air pump [1] a new mode of being was given to substances. With the aid of telescopes, distant objects were brought close to our eyes. Finally, what Newton discovered about light is equal to all that the curiosity of men could hope for in the way of something more exciting, after so many innovations.

Until Antonio de Dominis, the rainbow had seemed an inexplicable miracle; that philosopher discovered that it was a necessary effect of rain and sun. Descartes immortalized his name with the mathematical explanation of this most natural phenomenon; he tabulated the reflections of light in drops of water. There was something divine, then, in that sagacity of his.

But what would he have said if someone had informed him that he was mistaken about the nature of light; that he had no reason at all to declare that it was a globulous matter;

[1] Invented by Otto von Guericke by the middle of the 17th century. "In a tall glass well emptied of air," says Newton, "[small feathers] fall as fast as Lead or Gold."—*Opticks*, Book III, Part I, Query 28.

that it is false that this matter, spread throughout the universe, waits for the pressure of the sun in order to become manifest, as a blind man's stick does its work at one end when pressed at the other; that it is most certainly shot out by the sun and, in the end, transmitted from the sun to the earth in about seven minutes, whereas a cannon ball, maintaining the same speed all the way, could not make the trip in less than twenty-five years?

What would have been his astonishment if he had been told: "It is false that light is reflected directly in rebounding from the solid parts of a body; it is false that bodies are transparent when they have large pores; and a man is coming who will prove these paradoxes and who will anatomize a single ray of light more dexterously than the most skillful artist dissects the human body!"

That man came. Newton, with the help of nothing more than a prism, opened our eyes to the fact that light is an agglomeration of colored rays which, all together, produce the color white. A single ray he divides into seven, which, on a piece of linen or white paper, range themselves in order, one above the other and at unequal distances. The first is the color of fire; the second, lemon; [2] the third, yellow; the fourth, green; the fifth, blue; the sixth, indigo; the seventh, violet. Each of these rays, though sifted afterward through a hundred other prisms, will keep its color unchanged, just as gold, once refined, changes no more in crucibles. And, for more than sufficient proof that each of these elementary rays bears within itself that which makes what we call its color, take a small piece of yellow wood, for example, and expose it to the fire-colored ray: the wood is instantly tinted fire-color; expose it to the green ray: it becomes green; and so with the others.

What then is the cause of the colors we find in the world? Nothing other than the disposition of bodies to reflect rays of a certain sort and to absorb all the others. What is this hidden disposition? He shows that it is only the thickness of

[2] It is not known how red and orange become *couleur de feu* and *citron* in Voltaire.

the little parts of which a body is composed. And how is this reflection done? It used to be thought that the rays rebounded, like a ball, from the surface of a solid body. Not at all. Newton taught the astonished philosophers that bodies are opaque only because their pores are large, that light is reflected to our eyes from the heart of those very pores; and that the smaller the pores of a body are, the more transparent is that body. Thus paper, which reflects light when it is dry, suffers it to pass through when it is oiled, because the oil, filling the pores, makes them much smaller.

It is there, in considering the extreme porosity of bodies, each part having its pores, and each part of its parts having its own, that he shows that we are not at all assured of there being a cubic inch of solid matter in the universe: so far is our intellect from conceiving what matter is.

Having thus decomposed light, and in the brilliance of his discoveries having gone so far as to demonstrate the means of knowing a compound color by its primary colors, he shows that these primary rays, separated by the agency of the prism, are in their particular order because they are refracted in that order; and it is this property, unknown before him, of breaking in proportion, it is this unequal refraction of rays, this property of refracting red less than orange, and so on, that he names refrangibility.

The most reflexible rays are the most refrangible; from that he shows that the causes of the reflection and refraction of light are one and the same.

Wondrous as these discoveries are, they are only the beginning. He discovered how to observe the vibrations and agitations of light, which come and go endlessly, and which transmit light or reflect it according to the thickness of the parts they encounter. He ventured to calculate the thickness of the particles of air necessary between two object-glasses set one upon the other—one of them flat, and the other convex on one side—to produce such and such a transmission or reflection, and to make such and such a color.

From all these contrivances he found the proportion according to which light acts upon bodies and bodies act upon it.

He understood light so well that he determined the limits of the art of augmenting it and aiding our eyes with telescopes.

Descartes, with a noble confidence quite excusable in the heat of working on the early stages of an art practically discovered by him—Descartes hoped to see, with a spyglass, objects in the heavens as small as those we can discern on earth.

Newton showed, however, that we cannot go on improving dioptric telescopes, because of that very refraction and refrangibility, which, in bringing objects closer to us, causes too much dispersion of the primary rays. He figured out, in working with those object-glasses, the proportion of dispersion of red rays and blue rays; and, carrying the demonstration over into matters whose existence even was not suspected, he examined the inequalities produced by the figure of the glass, and by refrangibility. He found that if the plane side of the object-glass of a telescope, convex on one side and plane on the other, is turned toward the object, the imperfection owing to the construction and the position of the glass is five thousand times less than that caused by refrangibility; and that thus, it is not the figure of the glasses that makes it impossible to perfect the telescope, but the nature of light itself.

That is why he invented a telescope that works by reflection rather than by refraction. This new kind of telescope is very difficult to make, and not exactly easy to operate, but they say in England that a five-foot reflecting telescope magnifies as much as a refracting telescope a hundred feet long.

LETTER SEVENTEEN

ON INFINITY AND ON CHRONOLOGY

The labyrinth and the abyss of the infinite were another new territory surveyed by Newton, and it was he who gave us the thread by which we may find our way.

In this stunning innovation, Descartes again is found to be his precursor; in geometry he had been taking long strides in the direction of the infinite, but he stopped on the brink of it. Mr. Wallis, about the middle of the last century, was the first to reduce a fraction, by a perpetual division, to an infinite series.

Lord Brouncker made use of the series to square the hyperbola.

Mercator [1] published a demonstration of that quadrature. It was about this time that Newton, at the age of twenty-three, invented a general method of doing with all curves what had just been essayed with the hyperbola.

It is this method of submitting infinity everywhere to algebraic reckoning that is called differential calculus or fluxions and integral calculus. It is the art of exactly numbering and measuring that of which we cannot even conceive the existence.

In fact, wouldn't you think a man was making fun of you if he told you that there are lines infinite in extent that form an angle infinitely small? That a straight line, which is straight so long as it is finite, in changing direction infinitely little, turns into an infinite curve: that a curve may become infinitely less a curve? That there are squares of infinity, cubes of infinity, and infinites of infinity, of which the next-to-last is nothing compared with the last?

All that, which strikes us at first as excess of unreason, is

[1] Not the geographer, but Nicholas Kauffmann (c. 1620-87).

really the working of the human mind at its most delicately fine and most broadly encompassing, and the method of finding out truths till then unperceived.

Imposing as it is, this edifice is based on simple ideas. It is just a matter of measuring the diagonal of a square, of finding the area of a curve, of figuring out the square root of a number that in ordinary arithmetic hasn't any.

And, after all, so many orders of infinites ought not to shock the imagination more than that familiar proposition that one can always introduce more curves between a circle and its tangent; or that other to the effect that matter is endlessly divisible. These two facts were proved long ago, and are no more comprehensible than the rest.

Newton's claim to the invention of this famous calculus was for some time disputed. In Germany M. Leibniz was known as the discoverer of the differentials that Newton calls fluxions, and the integral calculus has been claimed by Bernoulli; but the honor of first discovery has remained Newton's, and to the others falls the glory of having made anyone doubt it.

It is thus that Harvey's right to the discovery of the circulation of the blood was contested, and M. Perrault's of the circulation of sap. Hartsoeker and Leeuwenhoek disputed the honor of having first seen the little grubs from which we come. Hartsoeker, again, disputed with M. Huyghens the invention of a new means of calculating the distance of a fixed star. We still don't know which philosopher [2] first solved the problem of the cycloid.

At any rate, it is through that geometry of the infinite that Newton arrived at the sublimest of discoveries.

I have still to speak to you about another work, one more within the grasp of the human race, and that yet shows the marks of that creative spirit which Newton carried into all his studies. This is a brand new chronology, for in all his undertakings he had to alter the accepted ideas of mankind.

Accustomed to bringing order out of chaos, he desired to

2 Torricelli, Father Mersenne, or G. P. de Roberval.

shine at least a little light on the place where ancient fables are confounded with history, and to fix an unsettled chronology. The fact is that there is no family, town, or nation that does not do what it can to push back its date of origin; in addition, the first historians were the most negligent of dates; books were then a thousand times less common than they are today; consequently, being less exposed to criticism, the earlier historians found it less inconvenient to deceive the world; and since it is clear that they fabricated events, it is quite probable that they fabricated dates as well.

Briefly, it seemed to Newton that the world was younger than the chronologists said it was by five hundred years. His idea was founded on the ordinary course of nature and on astronomical observations.

By the course of nature, here, is meant the length of each generation of men. The Egyptians were the first to make use of this uncertain mode of counting. When they wanted to write about the beginnings of their history, they counted three hundred and forty-one generations from Menes [3] to Sethon; [4] and, having no fixed dates, they estimated three generations at a hundred years. Thus from the reign of Menes to that of Sethon they reckoned eleven thousand three hundred and forty years.

The Greeks, before counting by Olympiads, followed the Egyptian method and even slightly extended the length of a generation, stretching it to forty years.

Now the Egyptians and the Greeks were out in their reckoning here. It is true enough that in the ordinary course of nature three generations cover some hundred to a hundred and twenty years, but three reigns are not likely to come to that number. It is most evident that in general men live

[3] Founder of the first dynasty of Egypt (c. 3315 B.C.)

[4] Or Sethos: King of Egypt about 700 B.C.(?). According to Herodotus he was the priest of Hephaestus and a scorner of the warrior class. As a result, when the country was invaded by the armies of Sennacherib he found himself reduced to rallying an army of artisans and small tradesmen.

longer than kings reign. So anyone who desires to write history without being provided with exact dates, and who knows that a nation has had nine kings, will be much mistaken if he estimates for these nine kings three hundred years. Each generation is about thirty-six years; each reign is about twenty, on the average. Take the thirty kings of England from William the Conqueror to George I. They reigned six hundred and forty-eight years, which, divided among the thirty, gives each king a reign of twenty-one and a half years. Sixty-three kings of France have reigned, each, on the average, about twenty years. So much for the ordinary course of nature. The ancients, then, were wrong when they made the duration of reigns generally equivalent to that of generations; because of it they got too high a total; because of that it is appropriate to cut their figures down a bit.

Astronomical observations seem to lend even greater aid to our philosopher; he makes a better figure fighting on his own ground.

You know, Sir, that the earth, besides its annual course that takes it round the sun from west to east in the space of a year, has another remarkable kind of motion, one entirely unknown until recently. Its poles show a very slow movement of retrogradation from east to west, which causes their position not to match with the same points in the heavens every day. That discrepancy, imperceptible in one year, becomes quite large in time, and at the end of seventy-two years is found to amount to a degree—that is, a three hundred and sixtieth part of the heavens. Thus, after seventy-two years the colure of the spring equinox, which passed through one fixed star, will be in the same relationship to another. As a result the sun, instead of being in that part of the heavens where Aries [5] was in the days of Hipparchus, is found in that part where Taurus was, and where Taurus used to be, the Gemini are now. All the signs of the zodiac have shifted; yet we still hold on to the ancient manner of speaking: we say that in springtime the sun is in the Ram, with that amiable condescension with which we say that the sun rises and sets.

[5] Or the Ram.

Hipparchus was the first among the Greeks to notice certain changes in the constellations in accordance with the equinoxes—or rather, he was the first to learn about it from the Egyptians. Philosophers attributed this movement to the stars, for at the time they were far from imagining the earth to be involved in such revolutions: they believed it to be in all senses immobile. And so they created a heaven to which they attached all the stars, and gave it a motion of its own that made it go toward the east, while all the stars seemed to make their daily journey from east to west. To this error they added a second that was much more important: they believed that the imaginary heaven of the fixed stars moved eastward by one degree in a hundred years. Thus they were mistaken in their astronomical calculations as well as in their physical system. For example, an astronomer would have said at the time: "In the days of such-and-such an observer, the spring equinox was in such-and-such a sign of the zodiac, at such-and-such a star; since then it has traveled two degrees; now two degrees are here equivalent to two hundred years; therefore that observer lived two hundred years before me." It is certain that an astronomer reasoning in this way would be wrong by exactly fifty-four years. That is why the ancients, doubly in error, invented their Great Year of a complete revolution of the heavens, taking about thirty-six thousand years. But the moderns know that that imaginary revolution of the heaven belonging to the stars is nothing else than the revolution of the poles of the earth, which is completed in twenty-five thousand nine hundred years. It should be said here, in passing, that Newton, in determining the figure of the earth, explained the reason for that revolution most happily.

Once all this is laid down, in order to establish chronology it remains to find at what star the colure of the equinox cuts the ecliptic in the spring nowadays, and whether some ancient cannot be found who has told us at what point the ecliptic was cut in his time by the same colure of the equinoxes.

Clement of Alexandria reports that Chiron, a member of the expedition of the Argonauts, observed the constellations during the course of that famous expedition, and fixed the spring equinox in the middle of Aries, the autumnal equinox in the middle of Libra, the summer solstice in the middle of Cancer, and the winter solstice in the middle of Capricorn.

Long after the expedition of the Argonauts, and a year before the Peloponnesian War, Meton observed that the point of the summer solstice was on the eighth degree of Cancer.

Now there are thirty degrees in each sign of the zodiac. In the time of Chiron the solstice was at the halfway point of the sign—that is, at the fifteenth degree; a year before the Peloponnesian War it was at the eighth: thus it had retarded by seven degrees. A degree amounts to seventy-two years: thus, from the beginning of the Peloponnesian War back to the Argonauts' enterprise, there is only a matter of seven times seventy-two, making five hundred and four years, and not seven hundred as the Greeks said. And so in comparing the state of the heavens today with what it was then, we see that the expedition of the Argonauts must be set about nine hundred years before Christ, and not some fourteen hundred years; and consequently the world is less old than we thought by about five hundred years.

In this way all periods are brought closer together, and everything takes place later than it is said to. I do not know whether this system will have much success, or whether people are going to resolve, on the basis of these ideas, to reform the chronology of the world. Perhaps it will strike the scholars as excessive to grant to one man the honor of having perfected physics, geometry, and history, all at once. That would be a sort of universal monarchy difficult for self-conceit to be comfortable in. Naturally, then, at the same time that very great philosophers attacked him on the subject of attraction, others fought his system of chronology. Time, which ought to show to whom the victory belongs, may only leave the dispute more doubtful.

PHILOSOPHICAL LETTERS

LETTER EIGHTEEN

ON TRAGEDY

The English, as well as the Spaniards, already had a theater while the French still had nothing but fair-booths. Shakespeare, who was reputed the Corneille [1] of the English, flourished about the time of Lope de Vega. He it was who created the English theater. His was a fecund genius, full of vigor, ranging from simple naturalness to the sublime, without the least glimmer of taste or the slightest knowledge of the rules. I am going to tell you something rash, but true: the greatness of Shakespeare has been the ruin of the English stage. There are such beautiful scenes, such grand and terrible passages scattered throughout those monstrous farces of his called tragedies, that these plays have always been put on with great success. Time, which alone makes the reputation of men, in the end makes their faults respectable. Most of the crude whimsy and the enormous extravagance of this author has, after two hundred years,[2] acquired the right to pass for sublimity. Almost all the modern authors have copied him; but what succeeded in Shakespeare is hissed in them, and you can imagine that the veneration people have for this ancient increases with their contempt for the moderns. It doesn't occur to them that he ought not to be imitated, and the poor success of his copyists only makes people think him inimitable.

You know that in the tragedy of the Moor of Venice, a most moving play, a husband strangles his wife on the stage, and that when the deed is done she cries out that her murder is most unjust. You know also that in *Hamlet* some gravediggers

[1] In another edition: "whom the English take for a Sophocles."
[2] Voltaire's hasty arithmetic.

drink and sing comic songs while digging a grave, and joke about the skulls they come upon in a style fitting to their profession. You will be surprised, however, to hear that this boorishness was imitated in the reign of Charles II, the reign of manners, the golden age of the fine arts.

Otway, in his *Venice Preserved,* introduces his senator, Antonio and Nacky, the courtesan into the midst of the horrors of the Marquis of Bedamar's conspiracy. The Senator plays with his courtesan all the monkey tricks of an old lecher, impotent and out of his head. He pretends to be a bull and then a dog; he bites the legs of his mistress, who kicks him and strikes him with a whip. This buffoonery, written for the vilest riffraff, has been cut out of Otway's play, but they have left in Shakespeare's *Julius Caesar* the jokes of the Roman shoemakers and cobblers who are brought on to the scene with Brutus and Cassius. The reason is that the stupidity of Otway is modern and that of Shakespeare is old.

No doubt you are objecting that up to now those who have said anything to you about the English theater, and especially about this famous Shakespeare, have shown you nothing but his faults, and that no one has translated any of those striking passages for whose beauties all faults must be forgiven. I reply that it is easy enough to recount in prose the errors of a poet, but extremely difficult to translate his fine verses. The scribblers who set themselves up as critics of celebrated writers all compile volumes; give me rather two pages that will acquaint us with a few beauties. For I shall always maintain with people of taste that there is more profit in a dozen lines of Homer and of Virgil than in all the critiques ever made on these two great men.

I have ventured to translate a few passages from the best English poets. Here is one from Shakespeare. Pardon the imitation for the sake of the original, and remember always when you see a translation that it is only a feeble print of a fine painting.

I have chosen the soliloquy from the tragedy of *Hamlet* that everybody knows and that begins with this verse:

"To be or not to be, that is the question."

Hamlet, Prince of Denmark, is speaking.

Demeure; il faut choisir et passer à l'instant
De la vie à la mort, ou de l'être au néant:
Dieux cruels! s'il en est, éclairez mon courage.
Faut-il vieillir courbé sous la main qui m'outrage,
Supporter ou finir mon malheur et mon sort?
Qui suis-je? qui m'arrête? et qu'est-ce que la mort?
C'est la fin de nos maux, c'est mon unique asile;
Après de longs transports c'est un sommeil tranquille;
On s'endort et tout meurt; mais un affreux réveil
Doit succéder peut-être aux douceurs du sommeil.
On nous menace, on dit que cette courte vie,
De tourments éternels est aussitôt suivie.
O mort! moment fatal! affreuse éternité,
Tout coeur à ton seul nom se glace épouvanté.
Eh! qui pourrait sans toi supporter cette vie,
De nos Prêtres menteurs bénir l'hypocrisie; [3]
D'une indigne maîtresse encenser les erreurs,
Ramper sous un Ministre, adorer ses hauteurs,
Et montrer les langueurs de son âme abattue,
A des amis ingrats qui détournent la vue?
La mort serait trop douce en ces extrémités;
Mais le scrupule parle et nous crie, "Arrêtez."
Il défend à nos mains cet heureux homicide,
Et d'un héros guerrier fait un chrétien timide . . .

Don't think that I have rendered the English word for word here. Woe to the makers of literal translations, who, in proceeding word by word, enfeeble the sense. This is where one can truly say that the letter killeth but the spirit giveth life.

Here is a passage from another famous English tragic poet, Dryden, who wrote in the time of Charles II. He was a more fertile than judicious author, who would have had an un-

---

[3] It seems that "to bless the hypocrisy of our lying priests" is not in Shakespeare.

blemished reputation if he had written only a tenth as much as he did. His great fault is to have wanted to be a universal genius.

The piece begins thus:

"When I consider life, 'tis all a cheat.
Yet fool'd by hope, men favour the deceit."

De desseins en regrets, et d'erreurs en désirs,
Les mortels insensés promènent leur folie.
Dans des malheurs présents, dans l'espoir des plaisirs,
Nous ne vivons jamais, nous attendons la vie.
Demain, demain dit-on, va combler tous nos voeux;
Demain vient, et nous laisse encore plus malheureux.
Quelle est l'erreur, hélas! du soin qui nous dévore?
Nul de nous ne voudrait recommencer son cours:
De nos premiers moments nous maudissons l'aurore,
Et de la nuit qui vient nous attendons encore
Ce qu'ont en vain promis les plus beaux de nos jours . . .[4]

It is in such detached passages that the English tragic poets have so far excelled. Their plays are almost all barbarous, devoid of decorum, of order, and of probability, but there are dazzling flashes in the middle of their night. The style is too bombastic, too unnatural, too much influenced by the Hebrew writers in all their Asiatic inflation. And yet one must admit that in hoisting the English language up to teeter on the stilts of the figurative style, they have raised the mind pretty high as well, though it goes at an awkward gait.

4   "When I consider life, 'tis all a cheat;
          Yet, fooled with hope, men favour the deceit;
          Trust on, and think to-morrow will repay:
          To-morrow's falser than the former day;
          Lies worse, and, while it says, we shall be blest
          With some new joys, cuts off what we possess.
          Strange cozenage! None would live past years again,
          Yet all hope pleasure in what yet remain;
          And, from the dregs of life, think to receive,
          What the first sprightly running could not give.
          I'm tired with waiting for this chemic gold,
          Which fools us young, and beggars us when old."
                    —*Aureng-Zebe*, Act IV, Scene I

The first Englishman to have made a reasonable play, and one written with elegance from beginning to end, is the illustrious Mr. Addison. His *Cato of Utica* is a masterpiece in its diction and in the beauty of its verse. The role of Cato is to my mind far superior to that of Cornélie in the *Pompée* of Corneille, for Cato is great without pomposity, and Cornélie —besides not even being a necessary character—has a propensity for gibberish. Mr. Addison's Cato seems to me the finest character on any stage, but the other roles in the play are out of keeping with this one. And the work as a whole, well written as it is, suffers from a spiritless love intrigue, which spreads over all a languor that kills it.

The custom of introducing love into dramatic works at random passed over from Paris to London about the year 1660, along with our ribbons and perukes. The ladies, who there as well as here adorn the theaters, will no longer tolerate on the stage any subject matter but love. The canny Addison was so weakly obliging as to bend the natural austerity of his character to suit the manners of his time, and spoiled a masterpiece to please the public.

Since Addison, plays have been more according to rule, audiences more particular, and authors more correct and less daring. I have seen some new plays that are very well behaved, but dull. It seems as if the English used to be born for the production of irregular beauties. The brilliant freaks of Shakespeare are a thousand times more delightful than modern sobriety. The poetic genius of the English until now has resembled a thick-spreading tree planted by nature, lifting its thousand branches as it pleases, and growing irregularly and with vigor. Prune it against its nature to the shape of a tree in the gardens of Marly,[5] and it will die.

[5] Reference is to a château, 10 kilometers from Versailles, built for Louis XIV by Mansart.

LETTER NINETEEN

ON COMEDY

I do not know how the wise and ingenious M. de Muralt, from whose pen we have had the *Letters on the English and the French,* managed, in writing of comedy, to confine himself to critical remarks on a comic writer named Shadwell. That author was sufficiently scorned in his time; he was by no means the poet of respectable people. His plays, enjoyed by the vulgar for a few performances, were disdained by all people of taste, and resembled so many plays I have seen in France that attracted the crowd and repelled readers, and that, as has been said,

"All Paris condemns and all Paris attends."

M. de Muralt ought, I think, to have spoken to us about an excellent author who was living then: Mr. Wycherley, who was long the declared lover of the most distinguished mistress [1] of Charles II. This man, who spent his life in the highest society, was perfectly acquainted with its vices and follies, and with the firmest of brushes painted them in their true colors.

He did a misanthrope, imitated from Molière. All the strokes of Wycherley are more bold and emphatic than those in our own misanthrope, but they are also less elegant and decorous.[2] The English author corrected the only fault in Molière's play, its lack of plot and interest. The English play is interesting and its plot is ingenious; it is no doubt too rude

[1] The Duchess of Cleveland.
[2] "Philosophy, liberty, and the climate lead to misanthropy. London, which has no Tartuffes, is full of Timons." Passage, in editions of 1756-84, within a larger passage substituted for our opening section of Letter XIX.

for our tastes. Here is a naval captain full of valor, frankness, and scorn for the human race. He has a wise and sincere friend whom he distrusts, and a mistress who loves him tenderly and on whom he does not deign to bestow a glance. On the other hand, he has put all his confidence in a false friend who is the most unworthy man alive, and has given his heart to the most perfidious coquette of her whole sex; he is positive that this woman is a Penelope, and this false friend a Cato. He goes away to fight against the Dutch, and leaves all his money, his jewelry, every last thing he owns, to this virtuous woman, and entrusts her to this faithful friend, on whom he counts so greatly. However, the true honest man, whom he so mightily distrusts, embarks with him; and the mistress he has not even deigned to look at disguises herself as a page [3] and makes the voyage without the captain's noticing her sex during the whole campaign.

Having blown up his vessel in a sea fight, the captain returns to London without support, with no ship and no money, accompanied only by his page and his friend, and realizing neither the friendship of the one nor the love of the other. He goes straight to the pearl among women, whom he expects to recover along with his money box and her fidelity: he finds her married to the honest rascal in whom he has confided, and his deposit no more chastely preserved than the rest. Our man has the greatest imaginable difficulty in believing that a virtuous woman could play such tricks; whereupon, the better to convince him, that good lady falls in love with the page, whom she determines to take by storm. But since justice must be done and, in a play, vice must be punished and virtue rewarded, we find as it turns out that the captain puts himself in the page's place, goes to bed with his faithless beauty, cuckolds his traitorous friend, runs him through the body, retrieves his moneybox and marries his page. You will note that the play has even been larded with a Comtesse de Pimbesche,[4] an old litigant, kinswoman of the captain, who is

---

[3] In the play, Fidelia is called "little volunteer."

[4] In Racine's Les Plaideurs. Voltaire refers here to Widow Blackacre.

quite the most amusing creature and the finest character on the stage.

Wycherley drew from Molière another play no less singular and no less audacious. It is a sort of *École des Femmes.*[5]

The main character in the piece is a rake, the terror of the husbands of London, who, to be more certain of success, decides to spread the word that in his latest illness the surgeons thought proper to make a eunuch of him. What with this fair name, all the husbands bring their wives to him, and the poor man has no longer any problem but choosing. He is particularly interested in a little country girl who is extremely innocent and amorous, and who cuckolds her husband with a simplicity worth more than the cleverness of the most expert of ladies. This play is not, if you must, the school of good behavior, but it is truly the school of wit and of good comedy.

A knight named Vanbrugh wrote some comedies that are even more amusing but less skillful. He was a man of pleasure, and a poet and architect into the bargain. It is held that he wrote as he built, with a somewhat heavy hand. He it was who built the famous Blenheim Palace, a weighty and durable monument to our unhappy battle of Hochstedt. If the apartments were only as wide as the walls are thick, this palace would be tolerably commodious.

In Vanbrugh's epitaph [6] we find the hope that the earth will not lie lightly on him, considering that he put such a pitiless load on it during his lifetime.

This knight, who came over to tour France before the war of 1701, was put in the Bastille, and stayed there some time,[7] without ever managing to find out what had caused our

---

5 *The Country Wife.*

6   Under this stone, reader, survey
    Dead Sir John Vanbrugh's house of clay.
    Lie heavy on him, earth! for he
    Laid many heavy loads on thee.
       —Abel Evans (1679-1737), sa-
        tiric poet and clergyman.

7 1690-92. The pretext for arresting him was that he had no passport, but some think that it was the vengeance of a woman.

Ministry to honor him with that distinction. He wrote a comedy in the Bastille; and, what seems to me very strange, in the whole play not a word is aimed against the country in which he suffered this outrage.

The Englishman who, of all his nation, has carried the glory of the comic theater to the highest point is the late Mr. Congreve. He wrote few plays, but all are excellent of their kind. The rules of the drama are rigorously observed in them; they are full of characters the subtleties of whose modeling are done with an extreme delicacy of touch; you are not subjected to the slightest unpleasantness in the way of humor; you find, throughout, the language of gentlemen with the behavior of knaves: which proves that he knew the world well, and that he lived in the midst of what is called good company. He was infirm and almost a dying man when I knew him. He had one fault, and that was not sufficiently to esteem his original calling of authorship, which had made his reputation and his fortune. He spoke to me of his works as if of trifles beneath his dignity, and told me, in our very first conversation, to consider him only as a gentleman living a most quiet life. I replied that if he had had the misfortune of being only a gentleman like any other, I should never have come to see him; and I was very much shocked at such misplaced vanity.

His plays are the wittiest and the most scrupulously written, those of Vanbrugh the gayest, and those of Wycherley the most vigorous.

It should be noted that none of these wits spoke ill of Molière. It is only bad writers among the English who have slandered [8] this great man. It is the bad musicians of Italy who scorn Lully, but a Buononcini esteems him and does him justice, as a Mead [9] thinks highly of a Helvétius and a Silva.[10]

England has other good comic poets, such as Sir Richard

[8] Referring to Thomas Shadwell.

[9] Physician to Newton and to Queen Caroline.

[10] The first was a physician, father of the philosopher; the second a Parisian doctor famous in Voltaire's time.

Steele and Mr. Cibber, an excellent comedian and moreover poet laureate, a title that seems ridiculous but that nonetheless brings with it an income of a thousand *écus* [11] and some handsome privileges. Our great Corneille did not have so much.

Don't ask, however, that I go into the least detail here about these English plays I am such a great admirer of, nor that I pass on to you a piece of wit or humor from the Wycherleys and Congreves. Laughter does not survive translation. If you want to know English comedy, there is nothing for it but to go to London, stay there three years, get a good grasp of English, and attend the theater every day. I find no great pleasure in reading Plautus and Aristophanes. Why? Because I am neither a Greek nor a Roman. The fineness in phrasing of witty remarks, allusions, the rightness or appositeness of things—all that is lost on a foreigner.

It is different in tragedy. There it is all a matter of great passions and of heroic foolishness consecrated by old errors of fable or of history. *Oedipus* and *Electra* belong to the Spaniards, to the English, and to ourselves, as well as to the Greeks. But good comedy is the speaking picture of the follies of a nation, and if you are not thoroughly acquainted with that nation you can hardly judge the painting.

11 The laureate received £100 a year.

LETTER TWENTY

ON PERSONS OF RANK WHO CULTIVATE LEARNING

There was a time in France when the arts were cultivated by persons of the first importance in the state. Courtiers particularly took them up, in spite of dissipation, of the taste for trifles, of the passion for intrigue—all deities of the nation.

It seems to me that today the vogue at Court is not for learning. Perhaps in a while the fashion of thinking will return. All that is necessary is for a king to wish it; you can do what you please with this nation. In England people have a habit of thinking, and learning there is more highly honored than in France. This fortunate condition is a necessary consequence of their form of government. In London there are about eight hundred persons who have the right to speak in public and to support the interests of the nation. About five or six thousand claim the same honor in their turn; all the rest set themselves up as judges of these latter, and each man may publish what he thinks about public affairs. Thus the whole nation is under the necessity of educating itself. You are always hearing them talk of the governments of Athens and of Rome; in spite of themselves they think they had better read the authors who have treated of those governments; this study leads naturally to belles-lettres.

In general, men have the kind of mind that corresponds with their calling. Why as a rule have our magistrates, our lawyers, our doctors, and many of the clergy more learning, taste, and wit than one finds in all the other professions? The answer is that it's really their calling to have a cultivated mind, as it is that of a business man to know business. Not long ago a very young English peer came to see me in Paris on his return from Italy; he had done a description of that country in verse as elegantly written as anything by Lord Rochester or by our Chaulieus, Sarrasins, and Chapelles.[1]

The translation I have made from it is so far from attaining to the energy and sprightly humor of the original that I am obliged seriously to beg pardon of the author and of those who understand English; however, since I have no other means of making known these verses of Lord———,[2] here they are in my own language:

> Qu'ai-je donc vu dans l'Italie?
> Orgueil, astuce et pauvreté,
> Grands compliments, peu de bonté,
> Et beaucoup de cérémonie;
> L'extravagante comédie
> Que souvent l'Inquisition [3]
> Veut qu'on nomme religion,
> Mais qu'ici nous nommons folie.
> La nature, en vain bienfaisante,
> Veut enrichir ces lieux charmants;
> Des Prêtres la main désolante
> Étouffe ses plus beaux présents.
> Les Monsignors, soi-disant grands,
> Seuls dans leurs palais magnifiques,
> Y sont d'illustres fainéants,
> Sans argent et sans domestiques.
> Pour les petits, sans liberté,
> Martyrs du joug qui les domine,
> Ils ont fait voeu de pauvreté,
> Priant Dieu par oisiveté,
> Et toujours jeûnant par famine.
> Ces beaux lieux, du Pape bénis,
> Semblent habités par les diables,
> Et les habitants misérables
> Sont damnés dans le paradis.[4]

1 Men of the world and writers of polished light verse. Chaulieu, an abbé, lived on into the eighteenth century.

2 John Lord Hervey (1696-1743).

3 Voltaire's note: "He doubtless means the farces that certain preachers put on in the public squares."

4 Literally translated into English:

"What then did I see in Italy? Pride, cunning, and poverty, elaborate compliments, little kindness, and a great deal of ceremony; the extrava-

Perhaps it will be said that these are the verses of a heretic; but every day people translate—and even quite badly—the

gant farce that the Inquisition often demands that we call religion, but that here we call madness. Nature, beneficent in vain, wishes to enrich this charming country; the desolating hand of priests smothers her loveliest gifts. The so-called great nobles, alone in their magnificent palaces, are illustrious idlers without money or servants. As for the little people, lacking liberty, martyrs of the yoke that masters them, they have made a vow of poverty, praying to God out of laziness, and always fasting for reasons of famine. These beautiful places, blessed by the Pope, seem haunted by devils, and the miserable inhabitants are damned in the midst of paradise."

Editors and translators of Voltaire have not known Hervey's original. A few years ago the Earl of Ilchester, in *Lord Hervey and His Friends, 1726-38* (London, 1950), published for the first time, from among the Fox papers at Melbury, a verse letter written in 1729 by Hervey to his wife, part of which, as anyone can see, Voltaire imitated in this chapter of the *Lettres Philosophiques*. Here are the passages of Hervey that apply.

> Throughout all Italy beside,
> What does one find but want and pride?
>
> Farces of superstitious folly,
> Decay, distress, and melancholy,
> The havoc of despotic pow'r,
> A country rich, its owners poor,
> Unpeopled towns, and lands untill'd.
> The nobles miserably great,
> In painted domes, and empty state,
> Too proud to work, too poor to eat.
> No arts the meaner sort employ,
> They nought improve, nor ought enjoy.
> Each clown from mis'ry grows a Saint,
> He prays from idleness, and fasts from want.
>
> .   .   .
>
> Whilst Milan's sons, oppress'd by power,
> Their fate in Paradise deplore,
> Ah! what avail her fertile plains,
> Her olives, vines, and swelling grains?
> A foreign Prince her wealth demands,
> Her vintage press'd by foreign hands,
> A foreign hand her harvest spoils;
> Vienna fattens on her toils."

The license taken by Voltaire in his version is characteristic and instructive.

verses of Horace and of Juvenal, who had the misfortune to be pagans. You are certainly aware that a translator is not answerable for the sentiments of his author; all he can do is to pray God for his conversion. And I don't fail to do that for the sake of his lordship.

ON THE EARL OF ROCHESTER
AND MR. WALLER

Everyone knows Lord Rochester by reputation. M. de Saint-Évremond has said a good deal about him, but he has acquainted us only with Rochester the famous man of pleasure, the rake; I should like to make known the man of genius and the great poet. Among other works that shone with that flowing imagination that was his only, he did some satires on the same subjects as those chosen by our famous Boileau.[1] I know nothing more useful for the perfecting of taste than to compare great geniuses who have tried their skill on the same subject matter.

This is how Boileau argues against the human reason in his satire on man:

> Cependant, à le voir, plein de vapeurs légères,
> Soi-même se bercer de ses propres chimères,
> Lui seul de la nature est la base et l'appui,
> Et le dixième Ciel ne tourne que pour lui.
> De tous les animaux il est ici le maître;
> Qui pourrait le nier, poursuis-tu? Moi, peut-être:
> Ce maître prétendu qui leur donne des lois,
> Ce roi des animaux, combien a-t-il de Rois?

> Behold him of his boasted reason vain,
> Drunk with the fumes of his distemper'd brain;
> Of nature he the base and corner-stone;
> The Heav'n of Heav'ns revolves for him alone;
> Of all that breathes on earth the sov'reign lord,
> And who will dare to doubt that sov'reign's word?
> Why, faith, my friend, that doubt belongs to me,
> This king of beasts, how many kings has he?[2]

[1] Voltaire here calls him Despréaux.

[2] Satire VIII. I quote the version found in the Smollett edition of Voltaire. It is better than John Oldham's.

Here, more or less, is how the Earl of Rochester expresses himself in his satire on mankind; [3] but the reader must continue to remind himself that these are free translations of English poets, and that the constraint of our versification and the delicate proprieties of our language do not allow of an equivalent for the impetuous license of English style.

Cet esprit que je hais, cet esprit plein d'erreur,
Ce n'est pas ma raison, c'est la tienne, Docteur;
C'est ta raison frivole, inquiète, orgueilleuse,
Des sages animaux rivale dédaigneuse,
Qui croit entre eux et l'Ange occuper le milieu,
Et pense être ici-bas l'image de son Dieu,
Vil atome importun, qui croit, doute, dispute,
Rampe, s'élève, tombe, et nie encor sa chute;
Qui nous dit: 'Je suis libre,' en nous montrant ses fers,
Et dont l'oeil trouble et faux croit percer l'Univers,
Allez, révérends fous, bienheureux fanatiques!
Compilez bien l'amas de vos riens scolastiques!
Pères de visions et d'énigmes sacrés,
Auteurs du labyrinthe où vous vous égarez,
Allez obscurément éclaircir vos mystères,
Et courez dans l'école adorer vos chimères!
Il est d'autres erreurs: il est de ces dévots,
Condamnés par eux-même à l'ennui du repos.
Ce mystique encloîtré, fier de son indolence,
Tranquille au sein de Dieu, qu'y peut-il faire? Il pense.
Non, tu ne penses point, misérable, tu dors,
Inutile à la terre et mis au rang des morts;
Ton esprit énervé croupit dans la mollesse;
Réveille-toi, sois homme, et sors de ton ivresse.
L'homme est né pour agir, et tu prétends penser!

And 'tis this very reason I despise,
This supernatural gift that makes a mite
Think he's the image of the infinite;
Comparing his short life, void of all rest,
To the eternal and the ever blest;
This busy puzzling stirrer up of doubt,
That frames deep mysteries, then finds 'em out,
Filling with frantic crowds of thinking fools,
The reverend bedlams, colleges, and schools;

[3] "A Satire against Mankind" (1675).

> Borne on whose wings, each heavy sot can pierce
> The limits of the boundless universe. . . .
> 'Tis this exalted power whose business lies
> In nonsense and impossibilities;
> This made a whimsical philosopher,
> Before the spacious world his tub prefer;
> And we have many modern coxcombs who
> Retire to think, 'cause they have nought to do.
> But thoughts were given for action's government;
> Where action ceases, thought's impertinent.
> Our sphere of action is life's happiness,
> And he that thinks beyond thinks like an ass.

Whether these ideas are true or false, it is certain that they are expressed with that energy which makes a poet.

I shall take good care not to examine the thing like a philosopher, or at this point to abandon the brush for the compasses. My sole purpose, in this letter, is to make known the genius of the English poets, and I am going to go on in the same style.

A good deal has been heard about the celebrated Waller in France. MM. de La Fontaine, Saint-Évremond, and Bayle have praised him, but people know nothing of him but his name. He enjoyed in London just about the same repute as Voiture did in Paris, and I think he deserved it more. Voiture appeared at a moment when we were emerging from barbarism and were still ignorant. Men wanted to be witty, but as yet were incapable of wit. They looked for turns of phrase instead of thoughts: imitation diamonds are more easily found than genuine ones. Voiture, born with a frivolous and facile talent, was the first to shine in that dawn of French literature. If he had come after the men who made the glory of the century of Louis XIV, either he would have remained unknown, or no one would have mentioned him except with contempt, or he would have reformed his style. Boileau praises him, but in his first satires, when his taste was not yet formed; he was young, and at the age when one forms one's opinion of men by their reputation rather than by what they are themselves. Besides, Boileau was often quite wrong, when he praised and when he censured. He praised Segrais, whom no one reads; he insulted Quinault, whom everyone knows by heart; he says not a word about La Fontaine. Waller, better than Voiture, was still not quite perfect. His elegant works are full of grace, but his negligence makes them dull, and falseness of thought often disfigures them. The English had not yet come to write with a fine accuracy.[4] His serious works have a vigor that one would not expect from the softness of his other pieces. He wrote a funeral eulogy on Cromwell, which with all its faults is accepted as a masterpiece. To understand this work you must know that Cromwell died on the day of an extraordinarily violent storm.

The piece begins thus:

> Il n'est plus; c'en est fait; soumettons-nous au sort:
> Le ciel a signalé ce jour par des tempêtes,
> Et la voix du tonnerre, éclatant sur nos têtes,
>   Vient d'annoncer sa mort.
> Par ses derniers soupirs il ébranle cette île,
> Cette île que son bras fit trembler tant de fois,
>   Quand, dans le cours de ses exploits,
>   Il brisait la tête des rois
> Et soumettait un peuple à son joug seul docile.
> Mer, tu t'en es troublée. O mer! tes flots émus
> Semblent dire en grondant aux plus lointains rivages
> Que l'effroi de la terre, et ton maître, n'est plus.
> Tel au Ciel autrefois s'envola Romulus,
> Tel il quitta la terre au milieu des orages,
> Tel d'un peuple guerrier il reçut les hommages:
> Obéi dans sa vie, à sa mort adoré,
> Son palais fut un temple, etc.

Upon the Late Storm, and of the Death of His Highness Ensuing the Same

> We must resign! Heaven his great soul does claim
> In storms, as loud as his immortal fame;
> His dying groans, his last breath, shake our isle,
> And trees uncut fall for his funeral pile;
> About his palace their broad roots are tossed

---

[4] *"avec correction,"* or, as they said in those days, "correctly."

Into the air.—So Romulus was lost!
New Rome in such a tempest missed her King,
And from obeying fell to worshipping.
On Oeta's top thus Hercules lay dead,
With ruined oaks and pines about him spread;
The poplar, too, whose bough he wont to wear
On his victorious head, lay prostrate there;
Those his last fury from the mountain rent:
Our dying hero from the continent
Ravished whole towns; and forts from Spaniards reft,
As his last legacy to Britain left.
The ocean, which so long our hopes confined,
Could give no limits to his vaster mind;
Our bounds' enlargement was his latest toil,
Nor hath he left us prisoners to our isle;
Under the tropic is our language spoke,
And part of Flanders hath received our yoke.
From civil broils he did us disengage,
Found nobler objects for our martial rage;
And, with wise conduct, to his country showed
Their ancient way of conquering abroad.
Ungrateful then! if we no tears allow
To him, that gave us peace and empire too.
Princes, that feared him, grieve, concerned to see
No pitch of glory from the grave is free.
Nature herself took notice of his death,
And, sighing, swelled the sea with such a breath,
That, to remotest shores her billows rolled,
The approaching fate of her great ruler told.

It was in reference to this eulogy on Cromwell that Waller
made to King Charles II the reply found in Bayle's dictionary.
The King, to whom Waller had just presented, according to
the custom of kings and poets, a poem stuffed with praise, reproached him with having done better for Cromwell. Waller
replied: "Sir, we poets succeed better in fiction than in truth."
That answer was not so sincere as the one made by the Dutch
ambassador who, when the same king complained that people
had less respect for him than for Cromwell, said, "Ah, sir, that
Cromwell was something else again."

My purpose is not to comment on the character of Waller
or of anyone else. I judge dead men by their works alone; for

me all the rest has been wiped out. I will only say that Waller, born at court, with an income of three thousand pounds a year,[5] never had the fatuous pride or the indifference to abandon his talent. The Earls of Dorset and of Roscommon, the two Dukes of Buckingham, Lord Halifax, and how many others, have not thought it beneath them to become very great poets and illustrious writers. Their works do them more honor than their names. They have cultivated letters as if they expected to make their fortune at it; they have, in addition, rendered the arts respectable in the eyes of the people, who, in all things, need to be led by the great, and who, however, pattern themselves less on them in England than anywhere else in the world.

[5] Translating the roundness of "60,000 livres," though £2,500 would be a nearer equivalent.

ON MR. POPE AND SOME OTHER
FAMOUS POETS

I wanted to speak to you of Mr. Prior, one of the most agreeable of the English poets, whom you saw in Paris as Envoy Extraordinary and Minister Plenipotentiary in 1712. I expected also to give you some idea of the poetry of Lord Roscommon, of Lord Dorset, and so on; but I realize that to do so I should have to write a big book, and that after a great deal of trouble I should only have given you a very imperfect idea of all those works. Poetry is a species of music: it must be heard before it can be judged. When I translate for you certain passages from these foreign poems, I take down for you, imperfectly, something of their music, but I cannot express the flavor of their song.

There is one English poem especially that I should despair of acquainting you with; it is called *Hudibras*. The subject is the civil war and the sect of Puritans held up to ridicule. It is *Don Quixote* and our own *Satire Ménippée* melted together; it is, of all the books I have ever read, the one in which I have found the most wit; but it is also the most untranslatable. Who would believe that a book that seizes upon all the absurdities of which the human race is capable, and that has more ideas in it than words, could not stand translation? The reason is that almost everything in it makes allusion to actual affairs: the brunt of the ridicule falls on the theologians, whom few people of fashion know much about; footnotes are necessary every moment of the way, and a joke explained is no longer a joke: every annotator of witticisms is a fool.

That is why the French will never understand very well the books of the ingenious Doctor Swift,[1] who is called the Rabe-

---

[1] "You will find in the same pacquet the second volume of m^r Gulliver, which by the by j don't advise you to translate. Stick to the first, the

lais of England. He has the honor to be a priest, like Rabelais, and, like him, to deride everything; but people do him great injury, in my humble opinion, to call him by that name. Rabelais, in his extravagant and unintelligible book, let loose an extreme jollity and an extremer impertinence; he poured out erudition, filth, and boredom; you will get a good story two pages long at the price of volumes of nonsense. Only a few persons of eccentric tastes pride themselves on understanding and esteeming this work as a whole; the rest of the nation laugh at the jokes of Rabelais and hold his book in contempt. He is regarded as chief among buffoons; we are annoyed that a man who had so much wit should have made such wretched use of it; he is a drunken philosopher who wrote only when he was drunk.[2]

Mr. Swift is Rabelais in his right mind and living in good company; it is true he has not the gaiety of the older man, but he has all the delicacy, the rationality, the selectivity, the good taste that are wanting in our Curé of Meudon. The style of his verses is unusual, almost inimitable; true wit and humor are his province in verse and in prose; but really to understand him you must travel a bit in his country.[3]

You can more easily get some idea of Mr. Pope; he is, I think, the most elegant, the most correct, and—which is in it-

---

other is overstrain'd. The reader's imagination is pleased and charmingly entertaind by the new prospects of the lands which Gulliver discovers to him, but that continued series of new fangled follies, of fairy tales, of wild inventions, palls at last upon our taste. Nothing unnatural may please long. T'is for this reason that commonly the second parts of romances are so insipid."—Voltaire to Thieriot, March 11, 1727 (Besterman 302).

2 He changed his mind about Rabelais: "I repent of having in times past spoken too ill of him." Voltaire to Mme du Deffand, April 12, 1760 (Besterman 8108).

3 In an additional passage dating from 1756, Voltaire remarks of the *Tale of a Tub* that, though Swift was ridiculing Catholicism, Lutheranism, and Calvinism, "he said, for his own reasons, that he did not touch Christianity itself. He claims to have respected the Father, while giving a hundred lashes to the three children. Some difficult people have thought that the switch was so long it reached the Father."

self a great deal—the most harmonious poet England has had.
He turned the harsh wheezings of the English trumpet into
the sweet sounds of the flute. He may be translated, because
he is remarkably clear, and because his subjects are for the
most part general ones, within the province of all nations.
The French will soon know his *Essay on Criticism* through
the verse translation the Abbé du Resnel is making.[4]
Here is a passage from the poem *The Rape of the Lock,*
which I have just translated with my usual freedom; for, once
again, I know nothing worse than to translate a poet word for
word.

Umbriel à l'instant, vieux Gnome rechigné,
Va, d'une aile pesante et d'un air renfrogné,
Chercher, en murmurant, la caverne profonde
Où, loin des doux rayons que répand l'oeil du monde,
La Déesse aux vapeurs a choisi son séjour.
Les tristes Aquilons y sifflent à l'entour,
Et le souffle malsain de leur aride haleine
Y porte aux environs la fièvre et la migraine.
Sur un riche sofa, derrière un paravent,
Loin des flambeaux, du bruit, des parleurs et du vent,
La quinteuse Déesse incessament repose,
Le coeur gros de chagrins, sans en savoir la cause,
N'ayant pensé jamais, l'esprit toujours troublé,
L'oeil chargé, le teint pâle et l'hypocondre enflé.
La médisante envie est assise auprès d'elle,
Vieux spectre féminin, décrépite pucelle,
Avec un air dévot déchirant son prochain,
Et chansonnant les gens l'Évangile à la main.
Sur un lit plein de fleurs négligemment penchée,
Une jeune beauté non loin d'elle est couchée:
C'est l'Affectation, qui grasseye en parlant,
Écoute sans entendre, et lorgne en regardant,
Qui rougit sans pudeur, et rit de tout sans joie,
De cent maux différents prétend qu'elle est la proie,
Et, pleine de santé sous le rouge et le fard,
Se plaint avec mollesse, et se pâme avec art.

Umbriel, a dusky, melancholy sprite
As ever sullied the fair face of light,

4 It was published in 1730.

Down to the central earth, his proper scene,
Repair'd to search the gloomy cave of Spleen.
Swift on his sooty pinions flits the Gnome,
And in a vapour reach'd the dismal dome.
No cheerful breeze this sullen region knows,
The dreaded East is all the wind that blows.
Here in a grotto shelter'd close from air,
And screen'd in shades from day's detested glare,
She sighs for ever on her pensive bed,
Pain at her side, and Megrim at her head.
Two handmaids wait the throne; alike in place,
But diff'ring far in figure and in face.
Here stood Ill-nature, like an ancient maid,
Her wrinkled form in black and white array'd!
With store of prayers for mornings, nights, and noons,
Her hand is fill'd; her bosom with lampoons.
There Affectation, with a sickly mien,
Shows in her cheek the roses of eighteen,
Practis'd to lisp, and hang the head aside,
Faints into airs, and languishes with pride;
On the rich quilt sinks with becoming woe,
Wrapt in a gown for sickness and for show.

If you were to read the passage in the original, instead of in this feeble translation, you would compare it with the description of Mollesse in *le Lutrin*.[5]

And that's the best I can do here on the English poets. I have touched a little on the subject of their philosophers. As for good historians, I don't know that they have yet had any; it took a Frenchman to write their history. Perhaps the genius of the English, which is either cold or impetuous, has not yet seized upon that artless eloquence which is History's, and that air it has that is both noble and simple. Perhaps also the spirit of party, which blurs the vision, has discredited all their historians: half the nation is always the enemy of the other half. I have found people who assured me that the Duke of Marlborough was a milksop, and that Mr. Pope was a blockhead, as, in France, certain Jesuits see in Pascal a small mind, and certain Jansenists say that Father Bourdaloue was only

5 See Appendix.

a babbler. Mary Stuart is a sainted heroine to the Jacobites; to the rest she is a debauchee, an adulteress, and a murderess; so in England they have scurrilous pamphlets and no history. It is true that there is at present a Mr. Gordon, an excellent translator of Tacitus, who is quite capable of writing the history of his country, but M. Rapin de Thoyras has forestalled him. All in all, it seems to me that the English do not by any means have such good historians as we, that they have no true tragedies at all, that they have charming comedies, admirable passages of poetry, and philosophers who ought to be the preceptors of the human race.

The English have greatly profited from literary works in our language; we ought in our turn to borrow from them, having lent to them before; the English and we did not come till after the Italians, who have been our masters in all things, and whom we have surpassed in some. I don't know which of the three nations deserves the preference; but happy the man who is able to savor their different excellences!

LETTER TWENTY-THREE

ON THE CONSIDERATION OWED
TO MEN OF LETTERS

Neither in England nor in any other country in the world does one find such establishments for the sake of the fine arts as there are in France. Almost everywhere there are universities, but only in France are there such serviceable encouragements for astronomy, for all aspects of mathematics, for medicine, for research into antiquity, for painting, for sculpture, and for architecture. Louis XIV immortalized himself by founding these institutions, and that immortality did not cost him two hundred thousand francs a year.

I confess that it astonishes me that the parliament of England, which went so far as to promise twenty thousand guineas to whoever should make the impossible discovery of the longitude, should never have thought of imitating Louis XIV in munificence toward the arts.

To be sure, merit finds in England other rewards more reputable in the eyes of the nation. Such is the respect that this people has for talent, that a man of merit there always makes his fortune. In France, Mr. Addison would have belonged to some academy, and would have been able to obtain, through the influence of some woman, a pension of twelve hundred livres; or rather, somebody would have done his business for him on the pretext that in his tragedy of *Cato* certain strokes had evidently been made against the porter of a man of position. In England, he was secretary of state. Mr. Newton was master of the Mint; Mr. Congreve held an important office; Mr. Prior was a plenipotentiary. Doctor Swift is a Dean in Ireland and is more highly esteemed there than the Primate. If the religion of Mr. Pope does not permit him to hold a place, it at least has not prevented his translation of Homer from bringing him two hundred thousand francs. For a long time in France I saw the author [1] of *Rhadamiste* on the verge of dying of hunger; and the son of one of the greatest men France has had, who was beginning to follow in his father's footsteps, would have been reduced to misery had it not been for M. Fagon.[2] What encourages the arts most in England is the prestige they enjoy: the portrait of the prime minister hangs above the fireplace in his office; but I have seen that of Mr. Pope in twenty houses.

Mr. Newton was honored during his lifetime and after his death as he should have been. The leaders of the nation disputed the honor of being his pallbearers. Go into Westminster Abbey. It is not the tombs of kings that one admires there, but the monuments erected by the gratitude of the nation to the greatest of the men who have contributed to its glory. You will see their statues, as one saw at Athens those of such men as Sophocles and Plato; and I am convinced that the mere sight of these glorious monuments has roused more than one mind and been the making of more than one great man.

People have even reproached the English with having gone too far in honoring simple merit; they have taken exception to their having buried the famous actress Mrs. Oldfield [3] in Westminster Abbey with nearly the same honors accorded Mr. Newton. Some have asserted that they made a show of honoring the memory of that actress to such a degree in order to make us feel more strongly the barbarity and cowardly injustice they reproach us with for having thrown out like rubbish the body of Mlle. Lecouvreur.[4]

But I can assure you that the English, in the funeral ceremonies of Mrs. Oldfield, whom they buried in their own Saint-Denis, consulted none but their own tastes. They are far

[1] Crébillon, whose masterpiece *Rhadamiste et Zénobie* was published in 1711. In old age he was given a pension by Mme de Pompadour.

[2] Louis Racine was granted certain offices through the help of Fagon (d. 1718), who was chief physician to the king.

[3] Anne Oldfield (1683-1730).

[4] Adrienne Lecouvreur (1692-1730). Voltaire's poem against the clergy's refusal to give her proper burial obliged him to leave Paris.

from attaching any infamy to the art of Sophocles and Euripides, or from cutting off from the rest of society those who devote their lives to reciting before them works that are the boast of the nation.

In the days of Charles I, and early in those civil wars begun by fanatical rigorists, who themselves were in the end their victims, a great deal was written against the theater, all the more because Charles I and his wife, the daughter of our Henry the Great, were extremely fond of it.

A certain Dr. Prynne, scrupulous to a fault, a man who would have thought himself damned if he had worn a cassock instead of a short coat, and who would have liked one half of mankind to have massacred the other for the glory of God and the propagation of the faith, took upon himself the writing of a very bad book against some rather good comedies that were put on quite innocently every day in the presence of the King and Queen. He cited Rabbinical authority and some passages from St. Bonaventura to prove that the *Oedipus* of Sophocles was the work of the Evil One, and that Terence was *ipso facto* excommunicate; and he added that Brutus, who was a very severe Jansenist, had doubtless assassinated Caesar only because Caesar, who was High Priest, had himself composed an *Oedipus;* finally he said that all who attended a play were excommunicates who abjured their chrism and their baptism. This was an outrage on the King and the whole royal family. The English then respected Charles I; they had no intention of allowing anyone to talk of excommunicating that King whose head they later cut off. Mr. Prynne was summoned before the Star Chamber and condemned to see his fine book burned by the hangman, and also to lose his ears. His trial appears in the public registers.

In Italy one takes good care not to cast any slurs on the Opera or to excommunicate Signor Senesino or Signora Cuzzoni. For my part, I should venture to hope that any number of bad books that have been published against the theater in France might be suppressed; for when the Italians and the English learn that we brand with the greatest infamy an art in which we excel, that we condemn as impious a play that is acted among the religious and in convents, that we dishonor plays in which Louis XIV and Louis XV have been actors, that we give Satan the authorship of works that have been reviewed by the strictest magistrates and acted before a virtuous queen; when, I say, foreigners hear about this insolence, this want of respect for royal authority, this Gothic barbarity that people dare to call Christian severity, what do you expect them to think of our country? And how can they conceive, either that our laws authorize an art that has been declared to be so vile, or that anyone should dare to brand with such vileness an art authorized by the laws, rewarded by sovereigns, cultivated by great men, and admired by nations; and that in the same bookshop Père Le Brun's declamation against our theater is to be found side by side with the immortal works of Racine, Corneille, Molière, and so on?

LETTER TWENTY–FOUR

ON ACADEMIES

The English had, long before us, an Academy of Science; [1] but it is not so well regulated as ours, and that perhaps only because it is older. For if it had been established after the Academy of Paris, it would have adopted some of its wise rules and perfected the others.

The Royal Society of London lacks the two things most necessary to man, rewards and rules. A seat in the Academy in Paris means to a geometrician, to a chemist, a small, secure fortune; on the contrary, in London it costs money to belong to the Royal Society. Whoever says, in England, "I love the arts," and desires to belong to the Society, belongs to it instantly. But in France, to be a member and pensioner of the Academy, it is not enough to be an amateur; one must be a scholar and contest the seat with rivals all the more formidable in that they are incited by fame, by interest, by difficulty itself, and by that inflexibility of mind that ordinarily comes of the persistent study of the calculative sciences.

The Academy of Science is wisely limited to the study of nature, and in truth it is a field broad enough to occupy fifty or sixty persons. The London Society indifferently mixes literature with physics. It seems to me that it is better to have a special academy for literature, so that nothing may be confused, and that one may not be confronted with a dissertation on Roman coiffures alongside a hundred new kinds of curves.

Since the London Society requires little order and offers no encouragement, and that of Paris is on another footing altogether, it is not surprising that the transactions of our academy are superior to theirs: well-disciplined and well-paid

[1] The Royal Society received its patent in 1660; the Académie des Sciences was founded in 1666.

soldiers must in the end prevail over volunteers. It is true that
the Royal Society has had a Newton, but it did not produce
him; few of his colleagues even understood him. A genius like
Mr. Newton belonged to all the academies of Europe, for all
had much to learn of him.

The famous Dr. Swift formed the plan, in the last years of
the reign of Queen Anne, of establishing an academy for the
language, after the example of the Académie Française. This
project was supported by the Earl of Oxford, Lord Treasurer,
and even more strongly by Viscount Bolingbroke, Secretary of
State, who had the gift of speaking extempore in parliament
with as much purity as Swift writing in his study, and who
would have been the patron and the ornament of that
academy. The members of whom it was to be composed were
men whose works will last as long as the English language:
there were Dr. Swift, Mr. Prior, whom we have seen here as a
diplomat, and who in England has the same reputation as La
Fontaine has among us; there were Mr. Pope, the Boileau of
England, Mr. Congreve, who can be called their Molière;
several others, whose names just now escape me, would all
have made that company flourish from its birth. But suddenly
the Queen died; the Whigs took it into their heads to hang
the patrons of the academy, and that, as you can well imagine,
was a mortal blow to literature. The members of this body
would have had a great advantage over those who first composed the French Academy; for Swift, Prior, Congreve,
Dryden, Pope, Addison, etc., had fixed the English language
by their writings, whereas Chapelain, Colletet, Cassaigne,
Faret, Perrin, Cotin, your first Academicians, were the dis-
grace of your nation, and their very names became so ridiculous that, if some tolerably good writer had the misfortune to
be born Chapelain or Cotin, he was obliged to change his
name. It would especially have been necessary for the English
Academy to propose for itself different pursuits from ours.
One day a wit of that country asked me for the Transactions
of the Académie Française. "It doesn't write up any," I replied, "but it has published sixty or eighty volumes of com-

pliments." He ran through one or two of them; he could never comprehend that style, though he had a thorough understanding of all our good writers. "All I get from these fine discourses," he said to me, "is a faint idea that the Member Elect, having declared that his predecessor was a great man, that Cardinal Richelieu was a very great man, Chancellor Séguier a sufficiently great man, and Louis XIV a more than great man, the Director then replies in the same words, and adds that the Member Elect may very likely be some sort of great man himself, and that as for him, the Director, he will hang on to his share."

It is easy to see by what fatality almost all these discourses have done so little honor to this body: *vitium est temporis potius quam hominis*.[2] The custom was imperceptibly established that each Academician should repeat these eulogies on his reception: it was a sort of law to bore the public. If one then tries to discover why the greatest geniuses who have become a part of this body have sometimes made the worst harangues, the reason once more turns out a simple one; it's that they wanted to shine, that they wanted to treat totally worn-out subject matter in some novel way. The necessity of speaking, the embarrassment of having nothing to say, and the desire to be witty are three things capable of making even the greatest man ridiculous. Unable to find any new thoughts, they looked for new turns of phrase, and spoke without thinking, like people chewing with empty mouths, trying to look as if they were eating, while perishing of starvation.

Instead of the rule of the Académie Française to publish all these speeches, by which, and by nothing else, it has become known, there should be a rule not to publish them at all.

The Academy of Belles-Lettres [3] has designed a wiser and more useful project, which is to present to the public a col-

---

[2] "It is more the fault of the time than of the man." Lanson traces the substance of the quotation to Seneca.

[3] Académie des Inscriptions et Belles-Lettres.

lection of Transactions full of research and scholarly critiques. These publications are already highly esteemed in foreign parts; one can only wish that they had gone rather deeper into some matters, and that others had not been treated at all. One could, for example, have done very well without some dissertation or other on the prerogatives of the right hand over the left, and various other studies which, under less ridiculous titles, are hardly less frivolous.

The Academy of Science in its researches, which are more difficult and of a more obvious utility, includes both the knowledge of nature and the perfecting of the arts. It is to be believed that studies so profound and so continuous, calculations so exact, discoveries so ingenious, prospects so extensive, will at last produce something that will work for the good of the world.

Up to now, as we have all observed together, it is in the most barbarous centuries that the most useful discoveries are made; it seems that the role of the most enlightened periods and of the most learned gatherings is to ponder over what ignorant persons have invented. We know nowadays, after the long disputes of Mr. Huyghens and M. Renaud, how to determine the most advantageous angle made by the rudder of a vessel with the keel; but Christopher Columbus had discovered America without even suspecting the existence of that angle.

I certainly do not infer from this that we should confine ourselves to working in the dark; but it would be well that physicists and geometricians joined practice to theory as much as possible. Is it necessary that what does most honor to the human mind should often be that which is least useful? A man with the help of good sense and the four rules of arithmetic becomes a great merchant, a Jacques Coeur, a Delmet, a Bernard, whereas a poor algebraist spends his life looking into numbers for ratios and for properties astonishing but useless, which will not so much as teach him what the exchange is. All the arts are pretty much alike in this: there is a point beyond which research becomes a matter of mere curiosity. These truths ingeniously arrived at but without utility are like stars that, fixed too far from us, give us no light.

As for the Académie Française, what a service it would render to literature, the language, and the nation, if, instead of every year publishing compliments, it reprinted the good works of the century of Louis XIV, purified of all the errors in language that have slipped into them! Corneille and Molière are full of them; La Fontaine is alive with them. Those that one could not correct would at least be noted. Europe, which reads these authors, would by their means gain a sure knowledge of our language. The purity of our language would be established forever; good French books, printed with such care at the expense of the Crown, would be one of the most glorious monuments of the nation. I have heard it said that M. Boileau once made the same suggestion, and that it was again put forth by a man whose wit, wisdom, and sound judgment are well known; [4] but this idea has had the fate of many another useful project, of being first approved and then ignored.

[4] "L'Abbé de Rothelin of the French Academy"—note in the Lockman translation (1733). F. A. Taylor adds, "He was government Censor at the time of the publication of the *Lettres Philosophiques*."

LETTER TWENTY-FIVE

ON THE *PENSEES* OF M. PASCAL

I send you the critical observations I long ago made on the *Pensées* of M. Pascal. Please don't compare me here to Hezekiah, who wanted to burn all the books of Solomon. I respect the genius and the eloquence of Pascal; but the more I respect them, the more I am persuaded that he himself would have revised many of these *Pensées,* which he had jotted down on paper as they came to him, so as to scrutinize them later on; and it is as an admirer of his genius that I combat certain of his ideas.

It seems to me that, on the whole, Pascal's motive in writing these *Pensées* was to show mankind in an odious light. He is dead set on painting us all wicked and miserable. He writes against human nature about as he wrote against the Jesuits. He attributes to the essence of our nature what pertains to certain men only. He eloquently insults the human race. I venture to take the side of humanity against this sublime misanthropist; I dare assert that we are neither so wicked nor so miserable as he says. Besides, I am quite convinced that if in the book he contemplated he had followed the plan that is manifest in his *Pensées,* he would have made a book full of eloquent paralogisms and of falsehoods admirably deduced. In fact, I think that all these books that people have been writing lately as proofs of the Christian religion are more likely to shock than to edify. Do these authors claim to know more about it than Jesus Christ and the Apostles? It's like trying to hold up an oak by setting reeds against it; you can take those useless reeds away without fear of doing any harm to the tree.

I have chosen with discretion certain thoughts of Pascal's; I put my replies below them. It is for you to decide whether I am wrong or right.

I.[1] The greatness and the wretchedness of man are so plain to see that the true religion must necessarily teach us that there is in him some mighty principle of greatness, and at the same time some mighty principle of wretchedness. For the true religion must know our nature perfectly, in other words must know everything about our nature that is great and everything about it that is wretched, and the reason for both. It must also explain to us the reason for the astonishing contrarieties that meet within us.

This way of reasoning seems both false and dangerous, for the fable of Prometheus and of Pandora, the androgynes of Plato, and the dogmas of the Siamese would explain these apparent contrarieties just as well. The Christian religion would remain no less true even if nobody drew these ingenious conclusions, which can serve no purpose but to make the wit shine.

Christianity teaches nothing but simplicity, humanity, charity; to wish to reduce it to metaphysics is to make of it a source of errors.

II. Let us examine all the religions of the world by this requirement and see if any besides the Christian satisfies it. Will it be that one taught by the philosophers who propose for the chief good a good that is within us? Is that the true good? Have they found the remedy for our ills? Is man cured of his presumption by being made equal to God? And those who have made us equal with the beasts, and who have given us earthly pleasures for the chief good—have they brought us the remedy for our lusts?

The philosophers taught no religion; it is not their philosophy that we are combatting. Never has a philosopher said he was inspired by God, for at that instant he would have ceased to be a philosopher and played the prophet. It is not a question of knowing whether Jesus Christ should carry the day against Aristotle; the point is to prove that the religion of Jesus Christ is the true one, and that those of Mahomet, the pagans, and all the rest are false.

---

[1] For the numbering of these items, see the Note on the Text, p. xv.

III. And yet without this mystery, the most incomprehensible of all, we are incomprehensible to ourselves. The knot of our condition draws its twists and its turns from the abyss of original sin, so that man is more inconceivable without this mystery than this mystery is inconceivable to man.

Is this reasoning, to say, "Man is inconceivable without this inconceivable mystery"? Why wish to go further than Scripture? Is there not some temerity in supposing that Scripture needs support, and that these philosophical ideas can give it any?

What would M. Pascal have replied to a man who said to him: "I know that the mystery of original sin is the object of my faith and not of my reason. I understand very well, without any mystery, what man is. I see that he comes into the world like the other animals; that giving birth is more painful to mothers the more delicate they are; that sometimes women and female animals die in childbirth; that there are sometimes badly formed children who live deprived of one or two senses and of the faculty of reason; that those who are best formed are those who have the liveliest passions; that self-love is the same among all mankind, and that it is as necessary to them as the five senses; that this same self-love is given us by God for the preservation of our being, and that he has given us religion to regulate this self-love; that our ideas are just or inconsequent, obscure or luminous, according as our organs are more or less sound, more or less finely made, and according as we are more or less impassioned; that in all things we depend on the air around us, and on the food we eat, and that in all this there is nothing contradictory. Man is not an enigma, as you picture it to yourself in order to have the pleasure of guessing it. Man appears to be where he belongs in nature, superior to the animals, whom he is like in his organs, inferior to other beings, whom he resembles probably in thought. He is, like all we see, a mixture of good and evil, of pleasure and of pain. He is provided with passions in order that he may act, and with reason that he may govern his actions. If man were perfect, he would be God, and these so-called contrarieties, which you call *contradictions,* are the necessary ingredients that enter into the composition of man, who is what he must be.

IV. Let us follow our own movements, observe ourselves, and see if we do not find the living traits of these two natures.

Would so many contradictions be found in a simple subject?

This doubleness of man is so obvious that some have thought we had two souls, for a simple subject to them seemed incapable of such diversity, of such sudden changes, from an overweening pride to a horrible prostration of spirits.

Our varying wills are not contradictions in nature, and man is not a simple subject. He is composed of a countless number of parts: if a single one of these parts is altered a little, it follows necessarily that all the impressions on the brain are altered, and that the animal has new thoughts and new desires. It is very true that we are at one time prostrate with grief, at another swollen with self-conceit: and that must be when we find ourselves in opposite situations. An animal that its master pets and feeds, and another that is slaughtered gradually, and with style, for purposes of dissection, have quite contrary feelings. So do we. And the differences in us are so little contradictory that it would be contradictory if they did not exist.

The fools who have said we had two souls could by the same token have given us thirty or forty; for a man in a great passion has often thirty or forty different ideas about the same thing, and must necessarily have them, according as that thing appears to him under different aspects.

This so-called *doubleness* of man is an idea as absurd as it is metaphysical. I would just as soon say that the dog that bites and fawns is double; that the hen, who takes such care of her little ones, and who afterward abandons them to the point of failing to recognize them, is double; that the mirror, which represents different things at one time, is double; that the tree, which is sometimes burdened with leaves and sometimes stripped of them, is double. I admit that man is inconceivable; but so is all the rest of nature, and there are no more contradictions to be seen in man than in everything else.

V. Not to bet that God exists, is to bet that he does not. Which do you choose, then? Weigh the gain and the loss in deciding to believe that God exists. If you win, you win all; if you lose, you lose nothing. Bet that he exists, then, without hesitation.—"Yes, one must bet; but perhaps I am laying too much."—Look, since there is equal risk of winning and losing, if you had only two lives to gain for one, you might still bet.

It is plainly false to say, "Not to bet that God exists is to bet that he does not"; for he who doubts and asks to be informed is certainly not betting, either for or against.

Besides, that article seems a bit indecent and childish; that notion of gambling, of losses and winnings, does not suit the gravity of the subject.

In addition, the interest I have in believing a thing is not a proof of the existence of that thing. You tell me you will give me dominion over the world if I believe you are right. I hope then with all my heart that you are right; but until you have proved it to me, I can not believe you.

Begin, one might say to M. Pascal, by convincing my reason. I have a stake, no doubt, in the existence of a God; but if, in your system, God has only come for so few persons; if the smallness of the number of the elect is so frightening; if I can do nothing at all by myself, tell me, if you please, what I have to gain in believing you. Have I not an obvious interest in being persuaded to the contrary? How can you have the effrontery to show me a limitless happiness, to which, out of a million men, hardly one has the right to aspire? If you want to convince me, set about it in another way, and don't go telling me about games of chance, about bets, about heads and tails; or, on the other hand, dismay me with the thorns you strew on the path that I not only wish to tread but must. Your reasoning would only serve to make atheists, if the voice of all nature did not cry out to us that there is a God, with a strength as notable as the weakness of these subtleties.

VI. When I see the blindness and misery of man, and these astonishing contrarieties that reveal themselves in his nature, and when I observe the whole universe to be mute, and man without light, given up to himself, and as if lost in this obscure corner of the universe, not knowing who put him here, what he has come to do, what will become of him when he dies, I am terrified like a man who has been carried, sleeping, on to a horrid desert island, and who awakes without any knowledge of where he is, and without any means of escape; and thereupon I marvel that one does not fall into despair at so miserable a state.

While I was reading that reflection I received a letter from a friend of mine,[2] who lives in a distant country. These are his words:

"I am here as you left me, neither gayer, nor sadder, nor richer, nor poorer, enjoying perfect health, with all that makes life agreeable, without love, without avarice, without ambition, and without envy; and so long as it all lasts, I shall boldly call myself a very happy man."

There are many men as happy as he. It is with men as with animals: a certain dog sleeps and eats with his mistress; another turns the spit and is every bit as contented; yet another runs mad, and we kill him. As for me, when I look at Paris or London I see no reason whatever for falling into this despair that M. Pascal is talking about; I see a town that in no way resembles a desert island, but is peopled, opulent, civilized, a place where men are as happy as human nature allows. Who is the wise man who will be ready to hang him-

---

2 Everard Fawkener (1684-1758), apparently from England, and in December, it may be, of 1728. He was to be knighted in 1735 and sent as ambassador to Constantinople, where he had been more than once before. In England Voltaire had lived for some time at Fawkener's house at Wandsworth.

self because he does not know how to see God face to face, and because his reason cannot unravel the mystery of the Trinity? One might as well despair over not having four feet and two wings.

Why make us hate our nature? Our existence is not so unhappy as they try to make us think. To look upon the universe as a dungeon, and all mankind as criminals who are going to be executed, is the idea of a fanatic. To believe that the world is a place of delight, where one should experience nothing but pleasure, is the dream of a Sybarite. To think that the earth, men, and animals are what they must be, according to the law of Providence, is, I believe, the part of a wise man.

VII. [The Jews think] that God will not leave the other peoples in darkness for ever; that a liberator of all will come; that they are here in this world in order to announce him; that they were expressly created to be the heralds of this great event, and to call upon all peoples to unite with them in expectation of the liberator.

The Jews have always been waiting for a liberator; but their liberator is for them and not for us. They await a Messiah who will give the Jews mastery over the Christians; and we hope that the Messiah will one day unite the Jews with the Christians. On this matter they think precisely the contrary of what we do.

VIII. The law by which this people is governed is altogether the most ancient law in the world, the most perfect, and the only one in any State that has been preserved without interruption. Philo Judaeus proves this in different places, and Josephus, admirably, in writing against Apion, where he shows that it is so old that the very word *law* was unknown to the most ancient authors until more than a thousand years later, so that Homer, who spoke of so many peoples, never used it. And it is easy to judge of the perfection of that law by simply reading it, when one will see that everything has been provided for with such wisdom, equity, and discrimination that the most ancient Greek and

Roman legislators, having some knowledge of it, borrowed from it their main laws: which is evident from those they call the Twelve Tables, and from the other proofs Josephus gives.

It is quite false that the law of the Jews is the most ancient, since before Moses, their legislator, they lived in Egypt, in the whole world the country most renowned for its wise laws.

It is quite false that the word *law* was not known till after Homer. He speaks of the laws of Minos. The word for law is in Hesiod. And if it were to be found neither in Hesiod nor in Homer, that would prove nothing. There were kings and judges; so there were laws.

It is also quite false that the Greeks and Romans took laws from the Jews. They could not have done so in the early days of their republics, for at that time they could not have known the Jews; they could not have done so in the days of their greatness, for then they had for those barbarians a contempt known to all the world.

IX. This people is still admirable in its sincerity. They preserve, with love and faithfulness, the book in which Moses declares that they have always been ungrateful to God, and that he knows that they will be even more so after his death; but that he calls heaven and earth to witness against them that he has told them so often enough; that one day God, in anger against them, will disperse them among all the peoples of the earth; that, since they have angered him by adoring Gods that were not their Gods, he will anger them by taking to himself a people that was not his people. Nevertheless, at the risk of their lives they preserve this book which dishonors them in so many ways. There is a sincerity without example in the world, nor with its roots in nature.

That sincerity has its examples everywhere, and its roots in nature only. The pride of every Jew finds reason to believe that it is not his detestable politics, his ignorance of the arts, his grossness that has been his undoing, but the wrath of God inflicted upon him. He thinks with satisfaction that it has taken miracles to down him, and that his nation is still the darling of the God who punishes it.

Let a preacher mount the pulpit and say to the French, "You are villains, heartless and ill-behaved; you were beaten at Hochstedt and at Ramillies because you could not defend yourselves"—he would be stoned. But if he says, "You are Catholics cherished by God; your infamous sins angered the Eternal, who delivered you into the hands of the Heretics at Hochstedt and at Ramillies, but when you returned to the Lord he blessed your courage at Denain"—these words will make the audience love him.

X. If there is a God, we must love only him and not the beings he has made.

We must love the beings he has made, and very tenderly; we must love our country, our wives, our fathers, our children; and it is so necessary to love them that God makes us love them in spite of ourselves. The contrary principles are fit only to produce barbarous dialecticians.

XI. We are born unjust; for each of us tends toward himself. That is against all order. We must tend toward the whole; and the slope down to the self is the beginning of all disorder in war, in government, in economy, etc.

That is according to all order. It is as impossible for a society to be founded and to survive without self-love as it would be to produce children without concupiscence, to imagine keeping alive without an appetite, etc. It is the love of ourselves that helps the love of others; it is through our mutual needs that we are useful to the human race; it is the foundation of all commerce; it is the eternal bond of men. Without it not an art would have been invented, not a society of ten persons formed. It is this self-love, which every animal has received from nature, that warns us to respect the self-love of others. Law regulates self-love, and religion perfects it. It is certainly true that God could have made creatures that were solely attentive to the good of others. In that case,

merchants would have gone to the Indies out of charity, and
the mason would have sawn stone to give pleasure to his
neighbor. But God has established things otherwise. Let us
not denounce the instinct he gives us, and let us make what
use of it he bids us to.

XII. [The hidden meaning of the prophecies] could not
lead into error, and there was only one people so carnally-
minded as that which could mistake it. For when goods are
promised in abundance, what prevented them from understanding true goods but their cupidity, which limited the
meaning to goods of this earth?

In good faith, would the most spiritual people on earth
have understood it otherwise? They were slaves of the Romans;
they awaited a liberator who would lead them to victory and
would make Jerusalem respected throughout the world. How,
by the light of their reason, could they see this conqueror,
this monarch in the poor and crucified Jesus? How could they
understand, by the name of their capital, a celestial Jerusalem,
they to whom the Decalogue had not so much as mentioned
the immortality of the soul? How could a people so attached
to its law, without superior insight, recognize in the prophecies, which were not their law, a God concealed in the form
of a circumcised Jew, who by his new religion destroyed and
made abominations of Circumcision and the Sabbath, sacred
foundations of the Judaic law? Once more, let us adore God
without trying to pierce the obscurity of his mysteries.

XIII. The time of the first coming of Jesus Christ is foretold. The time of the second is not, because the first had to
be hidden, whereas the second must be resplendent and so
evident that even his enemies will acknowledge him.

The time of the second coming of Jesus Christ was foretold
even more clearly than the first. M. Pascal had apparently
forgotten that Jesus Christ, in the twenty-first chapter of St.
Luke, says expressly: "And when ye shall see Jerusalem com-
passed with armies, then know that the desolation thereof is
nigh. . . . Jerusalem shall be trodden down. . . . And there

shall be signs in the sun, and in the moon, and in the stars
... the sea and the waves roaring ... for the powers of heaven
shall be shaken. And then they shall see the Son of man coming in a cloud with power and great glory."

Haven't we here the second coming distinctly foretold? But
if it has not yet happened, it is not for us to be so bold as to
question Providence.

XIV. The Messiah, according to carnal Jews, is to be a
great temporal prince. According to carnal Christians, he
came to dispense us from loving God, and to give us sacraments which will do everything without our help. Neither
the one nor the other is the Christian religion or the Jewish.

This article is really a stroke of satire rather than a Christian reflection. One can see that it's the Jesuits he is aiming
at here. But, truly, has any Jesuit ever said that Jesus Christ
came to dispense us from loving God? The dispute over the
love of God is purely a dispute over words, like most of the
other learned quarrels that have caused such intense hatreds
and such frightful woes.

Still another fault appears in this article. That is the sup-
position that awaiting a Messiah was a point of religion among
the Jews. It was only a consoling idea spread among that nation. The Jews hoped for a Liberator. But they were not required to believe in one as an article of faith. Their whole
religion was contained in the books of the law. The prophets
have never been regarded by the Jews as legislators.

XV. To examine the prophecies we must understand
them. For if one believes that they have only one meaning,
it is certain that the Messiah has not come; but if they have
two meanings, it is certain that he has come in Jesus Christ.

The Christian religion is so true that it has no need of
dubious proofs. Now if anything could shake the foundations
of that holy and reasonable religion, it is this opinion of M.
Pascal. If you believe him, everything in Scripture has two
meanings; but a man who had the misfortune to be incredu-

lous might say to him: "He who gives two meanings to his words intends to deceive the world, and such duplicity is punishable by law. How can you unblushingly attribute to God what is punished and detested in men? In fact, only consider with what scorn and indignation you treat the oracles of the pagans, because they had two meanings! Couldn't one say rather that the prophecies directly concerned with Jesus Christ have only one meaning, as those of Daniel, Micah, and others? Couldn't one even say that if we knew nothing at all about the prophecies, religion would be none the less confirmed?"

XVI. The infinite distance between body and mind shadows forth the infinitely more infinite distance between mind and charity; for charity is supernatural.

One assumes that M. Pascal would not have let this galimatias stand in his work, if he had had the time to write it.

XVII. The most evident weaknesses are strength to those who understand these things. For example, the two genealogies in St. Matthew and St. Luke. It is clear that that was not the result of collaboration.

Ought the editors of Pascal's *Pensées* to have printed this thought, the mere exposure of which is perhaps capable of doing harm to religion? What is the good of saying that these genealogies, matters fundamental to the Christian religion, contradict each other, without also saying what it is they may agree on? The antidote should have been presented along with the poison. What would be thought of a lawyer who should say, "My client contradicts himself, but that weakness is a strength to those who understand these things"?

XVIII. May we then no longer be reproached for lack of clarity, since we profess it; but may the truth of religion be recognized in the very obscurity of religion, in the little light we have on it, and in our indifference toward knowing it.

Strange tokens of truth, these that Pascal brings forward! What other tokens has falsehood? So in order to be believed all we have to say is, "I am obscure, I am unintelligible"! It would be a good deal more sensible to bring to our eyes only the light of faith, rather than this darkness of erudition.

XIX. If there were only one religion, God would be too manifest.

What! You say that if there were only one religion, God would be too manifest! Well! Are you forgetting that you say on every page that one day there will be only one religion? According to you, God will then be too manifest.

XX. I say that the Jewish religion consisted in none of those things, but only in the love of God, and that God condemned all the other things.

What! God condemned all that he himself had laid down to the Jews, with so much care and in such prodigious detail! Isn't it truer to say that the law of Moses consisted in both love and ritual? To reduce it all to the love of God smacks less of the love of God, perhaps, than of the hatred every Jansenist has for his Molinist neighbor.

XXI. There is nothing more important to life than the choice of a calling; chance decides it. Custom makes masons, soldiers, roofers.

What, after all, can lead to soldiers, masons, and all the kinds of manual laborers, except what we call chance and custom? Only in the arts of genius is the decision made by oneself. But in the kinds of work that everyone can do, it is most natural and most reasonable that custom should decide.

XXII. Let everyone examine his thoughts; he will find them always occupied with the past and the future. We hardly ever think of the present; and if we do, it is only to arrange the future by its light. The present is never our end; past and present are our means; the future alone is our object.

Far from complaining, we ought to thank the author of nature for giving us this instinct that ceaselessly carries us toward the future. The most precious treasure of man is that *hope* which allays our afflictions, and which paints future pleasures for us in our possession of present ones. If man were so unhappy as to be completely taken up with the present, we would not sow, we would not build, we would not plant, we would provide for nothing: we would lack everything in the midst of that false satisfaction. Could an intelligence like Pascal's espouse a commonplace as false as that one? Nature has settled it that every man enjoys the present in eating, producing children, listening to agreeable sounds, keeping busy his faculties of thinking and feeling; and that in coming out of these states—often in the middle of them, even—he thinks of tomorrow, for otherwise he would die of want today.

XXIII. But when I have looked closer, I have found that that aversion men have for repose, and to living with themselves, comes from a truly effective cause—that is, from the natural unhappiness of our weak and mortal condition, a condition so miserable that nothing can console us when nothing prevents us from thinking of it, and when we see only ourselves.

This phrase "see only ourselves" makes no sense.
What sort of thing is a man who doesn't act and yet supposedly contemplates himself? I say not only that such a man would be an imbecile, useless to society, but that such a man cannot exist: for what would he contemplate? His body, his feet, his hands, his five senses? Either he would be an idiot or he would make some use of all that. Would he stop at contemplating his faculty for thought? But he can contemplate that faculty only by exercising it. Either he will think of nothing at all, or he will think of the ideas he has already had, or else he will compose new ones. Now he cannot get ideas except from the outside. So there he is, necessarily occupied either with his senses or with his ideas; there he is, outside himself—or an imbecile.

Once more, it is impossible for human nature to stay in that imaginary torpor; it is absurd to think it can; it is lunatic to maintain that it can. Man is born for action as the sparks fly upward and as stone is earthbound. Not to be doing anything is the same for man as not to exist. All the differences are between gentle and turbulent occupations, dangerous and beneficial ones.

XXIV. Men have a secret instinct which impels them to seek for amusement and occupation outside themselves, an instinct that comes from their sense of endless misery; and they have another secret instinct, a remnant of the greatness of their original nature, which tells them that happiness is to be found only in quietude.

That secret instinct, being the first principle and the necessary foundation of society, comes rather from the goodness of God, and it is more the instrument of our happiness than a sense of our misery. I don't know what our first fathers did in the terrestrial paradise; but if each of them thought only of himself, the survival of the human race was certainly in peril. Isn't it absurd to think that they had perfect senses— that is, perfect instruments of action, for the unique purpose of contemplation? And isn't it amusing that thinking heads should imagine that indolence is a title of greatness, and action a lowering of our nature?

XXV. That is why, when Cineas [3] said to Pyrrhus, who proposed to take his ease with his friends once he had conquered a large part of the world, that he would do better to bring his happiness closer by taking that ease now rather than taking so much trouble to get to it, he gave a sort of advice that ran into great difficulties, and was hardly more reasonable than the plan of the young man of ambition. Both of them supposed that man can be content with himself and his present goods, without filling the emptiness of his heart with imaginary hopes—which is false. Pyrrhus could not have been content either before or after conquering the world.

The example of Cineas is good enough in the satires of Boileau, but not in a book of philosophy. A wise king can be

[3] See Boileau, *"Epitre au Roi"* and Plutarch, *"Pyrrhus."*

happy at home; and if Pyrrhus is presented to us as a fool, that means nothing where the rest of mankind are concerned.

XXVI. We must realize that man is so wretched that he would grow bored even without the remotest cause of boredom, from the peculiar nature of his condition.

On the contrary, man is most happy in this regard, and we are most obliged to the author of nature for having attached boredom to inaction, so as to force us to be useful to our neighbor and to ourselves.

XXVII. How does it happen that this man who recently lost his only son and who, crushed with lawsuits and quarrels, was so full of trouble this morning, has now forgotten it all? Don't be surprised: he is busy guessing where a stag will pass, that his dogs have been ardently pursuing for six hours. That is all man needs, however full of grief he may be. If one can persuade him to take part in some sort of diversion, he will be happy for as long as he does so.

That man is doing wonderfully well. Dissipation is a surer remedy for pain than quinine for fever. Let's not blame nature, which is always ready to come to our aid.

XXVIII. Imagine a number of men in chains, and all condemned to death, where some of them being every day slaughtered in the sight of the others, those who remain see their own state in that of their fellows, and looking upon one another sorrowfully and without hope, wait their turn. This is a picture of the condition of man.

This comparison is surely not a just one. Chained wretches who are butchered one after the other are wretched not only because they suffer, but because they undergo what other men are spared. It is not naturally a man's lot to be either chained or butchered; but all men are made, like animals and plants, to grow, to live a certain length of time, to reproduce their kind, and to die. In a satire you can emphasize the bad side of man as much as you please, but the moment you look at the thing reasonably you must admit that of all the animals man is the most perfect, the most happy, and the one that lives longest. Instead, then, of being surprised and grieved at the unhappiness and brevity of our life, we ought to be surprised and pleased at our happiness and how long we live. To argue merely as a philosopher, I dare say there is a good deal of pride and temerity in maintaining that we ought by nature to be better off than we are.

XXIX. Among the pagans, the wise men who said there was only one God were persecuted, the Jews hated, and the Christians even more so.

They were sometimes persecuted, just as a man would be today who came to teach us to worship a God independently of the accepted cult. Socrates was not condemned for having said, "There is only one God," but for having set himself against the country's outward forms of worship, and for having most inopportunely made some powerful enemies. As for the Jews, they were hated not because they believed in only one God but because they had a ridiculous hatred of other nations, because they were barbarians who pitilessly massacred their conquered enemies, because this base people, superstitious, ignorant, cut off from the arts, cut off from commerce, despised the peoples that were most civilized. As for the Christians, they were hated by the pagans because they tended to overthrow both religion and empire—which they finally succeeded in doing, as the Protestants made themselves masters of the same countries wherein they had long been hated, persecuted, and massacred.

XXX. The faults of Montaigne are great. He is full of dirt and impropriety. That kind of thing is worthless. His opinions on self-destruction and on death are horrible.

Montaigne speaks as a philosopher, not as a Christian: he gives the pros and cons of self-destruction. Speaking philosophically, what harm does a man do to society who departs from it when he can no longer serve it? An old man has the stone and suffers intolerable pain. He is told, "If you don't have yourself cut, you are going to die; if you are cut, you will be able to continue your dotage, to dribble, and shuffle

along for a year, a burden to yourself and to others." I suppose
the old fellow would choose to be no longer a burden to anybody. This is pretty much the kind of circumstance Montaigne
is talking about.

XXXI. How many stars have telescopes revealed to us
that did not exist for our philosophers of old! We used to
boldly attack the Scriptures on what is said there in so many
passages about the great number of stars. "There are only
a thousand and twenty-two," we said. "We know it."

It is certain that Holy Scripture, in questions of natural
philosophy, always adjusted itself to the prevailing opinion;
thus it assumes that the earth is immobile, that the sun moves,
etc. It is by no means from any astronomical subtlety that it
says the stars are innumerable, but to be in agreement with
the ideas of ordinary people. As a matter of fact, though our
eyes can discern only about a thousand and twenty-two stars,
nevertheless when we stare fixedly at the sky, dazzled, we think
we see an infinity of them. Scripture, then, speaks in accordance with this vulgar prejudice, for Scripture has not been
given us in order to make physicists of us; and there is every
indication that God did not reveal either to Habakkuk or to
Baruch or to Micah that one day an Englishman named Flam-
steed would put in his catalogue more than seven thousand
stars seen through the telescope.

XXXII. Is it courage in a dying man, in all his weakness
and agony, to affront an all-powerful and eternal God?

That has never happened; and only in a violent fit of
delirium could a man say, "I believe in a God, and I defy
him."

XXXIII. I willingly believe the histories whose witnesses
get themselves killed.

The difficulty is not only to know whether one is to believe
witnesses who die to support their testimony, as so many
fanatics have done, but whether these witnesses have in actual
fact died for that reason; whether their testimonies have been

preserved; whether they lived in the countries where it is said they died. Why did Josephus, born at the time of the death of Christ; Josephus, enemy of Herod; Josephus, not much attached to Judaism—why did he not say a word about all that? There is something that M. Pascal would have successfully unraveled, as so many eloquent writers have done since.

XXXIV. The sciences have two extremes which meet. The first is the pure natural ignorance that all men are born in; the other extreme is that which great souls arrive at, who, having run through all that men can know, find that they know nothing, and meet in that ignorance from which they first set forth.

This thought is a pure sophism, and its falseness consists in the word *ignorance* which he uses in two different senses. One who can neither read nor write is an ignorant person; but a mathematician, because he is ignorant of the principles hidden in nature, is not at the same point of ignorance from which he departed when he began to learn to read. Mr. Newton did not know why a man's arm moves when he wants it to, but he was not for that reason less learned about other things. One who does not know Hebrew, and who does know Latin, is learned in comparison with one who only knows French.

XXXV. It is not happiness to be able to find delight in diversion, for the latter comes from elsewhere and from outside; and thus it is dependent, and consequently subject to be disturbed by a thousand accidents that bring inevitable sorrows.

That man is at present happy who is experiencing pleasure, and that pleasure can only come from outside. We cannot have either sensations or ideas except through external objects, as we cannot nourish our body except by introducing into it foreign substances that change into our own.

XXXVI. Extreme intelligence is accused of madness, like the extreme want of it. Nothing is thought good but mediocrity.

It is not extreme intelligence but extreme vivacity and copiousness of mind that is accused of madness. Extreme intelligence is extreme exactness, extreme subtlety, extreme scope—diametrically opposed to madness.

Extreme *want of intelligence* is a deficiency in apprehension, an emptiness of ideas; this is not madness, it is stupidity. Madness is a derangement of the organs, which shows a number of objects too fast, or which holds the imagination on a single one with too much concentration and violence.

Nor is it mediocrity that is thought good, but the keeping away from the two opposite vices; it is what is called *the happy medium,* and not *mediocrity.*

XXXVII. If our condition were truly a happy one, it would not be necessary to divert ourselves from the thought of it.

Our condition is precisely to think about external objects, with which we have a necessary connection. It is false that one can divert a man from thinking about the human condition; for, to whatever he applies his mind, he applies it to something necessarily bound up with the human condition. And once again, to think about oneself abstracted from natural objects is to think of nothing whatever. One had best consider that carefully.

Far from preventing a man from thinking of his condition, one never converses with him about anything but the delights of that condition. One talks to a learned man about fame and learning; to a prince, about what is related to his greatness; to every man one talks of pleasure.

XXXVIII. The great and the humble have the same troubles, the same quarrels, and the same passions. But one group are at the top of the wheel, and the other close to the center—and thus less disturbed by the same movements.

It is false that the humble are less disturbed than the great; on the contrary, their despair is more acute because they have fewer resources. Of a hundred Londoners who kill themselves,

there are ninety-nine from the lower classes, and scarcely one
of high station. The comparison of the wheel is ingenious and
false.

XXXIX. Men are not taught to be upright men, and are
taught everything else; yet they pride themselves on nothing
so much as that. So they pride themselves only on knowing
the one thing they have not learned.

Men are taught to be upright men, and, if they were not,
few would manage to be. Let your son, in his childhood, take
everything he finds within his grasp, and at fifteen he will be
a highwayman. Praise him for having told a lie, and he will
become a false witness. Pamper his concupiscence, and he will
surely be a libertine. Everything is taught to men—virtue, religion.

XL. What a stupid project Montaigne had of painting
his own portrait! And this not in passing, and against his
maxims, since everyone makes mistakes, but by means of
his maxims themselves, and by his first and main purpose.
For to say silly things by chance and through weakness is
an ordinary failing, but to say them by design—and the
kinds of things he says—it's that that is intolerable.

What a charming project Montaigne had of painting his
portrait, artlessly, as he has done! For he has painted a picture of human nature. And what a paltry project, that of
Nicole, of Malebranche, of Pascal, to decry Montaigne!

XLI. When I have considered how it is that one puts so
much faith in so many impostors who say they have remedies, to the point that one often puts one's life in their
hands, it has seemed to me that the true reason is that there
are real remedies. For it could hardly be possible there
should be so many false ones, and that so much faith should
be placed in them, if there were no real ones. If there never
had been any, and all evils had been incurable, it is impossible that men should have imagined they could give
remedies, and even more so that so many others could have
put faith in those who boasted they had such remedies. Just
as if a man boasted he could keep people from dying, nobody would believe him, because there is no example of

such a thing. But, since there have been numbers of remedies that have been verified by the actual knowledge of the greatest men, men's belief has been won over, for since the thing cannot be denied in general (there being particular results which are true), the people, unable to distinguish which among these particular effects are the true ones, believe them all. In the same way, the reason why people believe in so many lunar influences that are untrue is that there are true ones, like the ebb and flow of the sea.

So it also seems clear to me that there are so many false miracles, false revelations, sorceries, only because there are true ones.

It strikes me that human nature can stumble into falsity without the help of truth. A thousand false influences were imputed to the moon before anyone imagined the slightest veritable relationship between it and the tides of the sea. The first man who was ever ill believed, without any difficulty, in the first charlatan. Nobody has seen any werewolves or wizards, and many people have believed in them. Nobody has seen any transmutation of metals, and a number have been ruined by believing in the philosopher's stone. Did the Romans, the Greeks, all the pagans believe in the false miracles with which they were inundated only because they had seen true ones?

XLII. The harbor guides those who are in a ship, but where shall we find this fixed point in morality?

In that single maxim accepted by all nations: "Do not do to others what you would not like to have done to you."

XLIII. *Ferox gens nullam esse vitam sine armis putat.*[4] They prefer death to peace; the others prefer death to war. Any opinion can be preferred to life, the love of which seems so strong and so natural.

It was of the Catalans that Tacitus said that; but there is no nation of whom it has been said, or could be said, "It prefers death to war."

[4] *Rati* rather than *putat.* "A savage nation who count life worthless without arms."—Livy, XXXIV, xvii.

XLIV. The more intellect one has, the more original men one finds. Ordinary people see no difference between men.

There are very few truly original men. Almost all behave, think, and feel according to the influence of custom and education. Nothing is so rare as a mind that strikes out on a new path. But of that crowd of men who walk together, each has little differences in bearing that fine eyes can perceive.

XLV. There are then two kinds of mind: the one penetrates acutely and profoundly into the conclusions from premises, and that is the exact mind; the other comprehends a great number of premises without confusing them, and that is the geometrical mind.

Present usage, I believe, calls the methodical and logical mind the geometrical one.

XLVI. Death is easier to bear without thinking of it than the thought of death without danger.

One cannot say that a man bears death easily or uneasily, if he does not think of it at all. Whoever feels nothing bears nothing.

XLVII. We suppose that all men conceive the objects they meet, and are sensible of them, in the same way; but we suppose this quite gratuitously, for we have no proof of it. I do see that we apply the same words to the same occasions, and that every time two men see snow, for example, they both express their sight of this same object by means of the same words, both saying that it is white; and from this conformity of application we draw a powerful conjecture of conformity of idea. But it is not absolutely convincing, though there are grounds for betting on the affirmative.

It was not the color white that should have been brought forth as proof. White, which is a combination of all rays, appears bright to everybody, dazzles a bit in the long run, has the same effect on all eyes. But one might say that perhaps the other colors are not perceived by all eyes in the same way.

XLVIII. All our reasoning reduces to this: the surrender to feeling.

Our reasoning reduces to the surrender to feeling in matters of taste, not in matters of science.

XLIX. Those who judge a work by rule are to the rest as those who have a watch are to those who have not. The one says, "We have been here for two hours"; the other says, "Only three quarters of an hour." I look at my watch; I say to the one, "You are bored," and to the other, "Time flies for you."

In works of taste, in music, in poetry, in painting, taste takes the place of the watch, and he who judges them only by rules, judges badly.

L. Caesar was too old, I think, to set out to amuse himself by conquering the world. Such an amusement was good enough for Alexander; he was a young man difficult to stop. But Caesar should have been more mature.

People generally suppose that Alexander and Caesar left home with the purpose of conquering the world. That isn't the way it was. Alexander succeeded Philip in the generalship of Greece, and was charged with the just undertaking of avenging the injuries inflicted on the Greeks by the king of Persia. He beat the common enemy and pushed his conquests as far as India because the realm of Darius extended to India —just as the Duke of Marlborough would have come as far as Lyons, if it had not been for Marshal de Villars.

As for Caesar, he was one of the leaders of the republic. He quarreled with Pompey, as the Jansenists with the Molinists; and then it was a question of which one would exterminate himself. A single battle, in which not ten thousand men were killed, decided the whole thing.

For the rest, M. Pascal's *pensée* is perhaps false in every sense. It took maturity in Caesar to disentangle himself from so many plots; and it is astonishing that Alexander, at his age, should have renounced pleasure to pursue so painful a war.

LI. It is an amusing thing to consider that there are people in the world who, after renouncing all the laws of God and nature, have made new ones for themselves which they obey to the letter, as, for example, thieves, etc.

That is even more useful than amusing to consider, for it proves that no society of men can subsist for a single day without rules.

LII. Man is neither an angel nor a beast; and as ill-luck will have it, whoever tries to play the angel plays the beast.

Whoever tries to destroy the passions, instead of regulating them, tries to play the angel.

LIII. A horse does not try to be admired by its companions. One sees among them some sort of rivalry in running, but it is of no consequence; for, once in the stable, the one who is heaviest and least well set up does not because of this give up his oats to another. It is different among men. Their virtue seems to them not enough in itself, and they are not satisfied if it gives them no advantage over others.

Neither does the least well set up man give up his bread to his betters, but the strongest takes it away from the weakest; and among animals and men the big ones eat up the little ones.

LIV. If man began by studying himself, he would see how incapable he is of going beyond himself. How could a part comprehend the whole? He will hope perhaps to know at least the parts to which he bears some proportion. But the parts of the world are all so closely connected and linked one with another that I believe it impossible to know one without the other and without the whole.

Man should not be turned aside from his search for what is useful to him through any consideration that he is unable to know everything.

Non possis oculo quantum contendere Lynceus, Non tamen idcirco contemnas lippus inungi.[5]

[5] "Though your eyes may not be as far-seeing as those of Lynceus, you do not scorn to anoint them when they are sore." Horace, *Epistles* I. 1, 28.

We know many truths; we have made many useful inventions. Let us console ourselves for not knowing the possible connections between a spider and the rings of Saturn, and continue to examine what is within our reach.

LV. If lightning fell on low places, the poets and those who only know how to reason about things of that sort would lack proofs.

A comparison is not a proof either in poetry or in prose: in poetry it serves as embellishment, and in prose it serves to clarify things and make them more palpable. The poets who have compared the misfortunes of the great with lightning striking mountains, would make comparisons to the contrary if the contrary happened.

LVI. It is that compound of body and of spirit which has caused almost all philosophers to mix up the ideas of things, and attribute to body what belongs only to the spirit, and to spirit what is only consonant with body.

If we knew what spirit is, we could complain that philosophers have attributed to it what does not belong to it. But we do not know what either spirit or body is. We haven't the slightest conception of the one, and we have only very imperfect ideas of the other. Thus we cannot know the limits of either.

LVII. As we say *poetical beauty,* so we ought also to say *geometrical beauty* and *medical beauty.* But we do not; and the reason is that we know very well what the purpose of geometry is, and what the purpose of medicine, but we do not know in what consists the pleasure which is the purpose of poetry. We do not know what that natural model is that we are to imitate; and, lacking that knowledge, we have invented certain bizarre terms: *golden age, marvel of our day, fatal laurel, fair luminary,* etc.; and we call this jargon poetical beauty. But whoever can imagine a woman dressed after this model, will see a pretty maiden covered with mirrors and chains of brass.

This is all wrong. We should not speak of *geometrical* or *medical beauty* because a theorem and a purge do not affect the senses agreeably, and because we give the name of *beauty* only to the things that charm the senses, like music, painting, eloquence, poetry, fine architecture, etc.

The reason M. Pascal adduces is just as false. We know very well in what the object of poetry consists: it consists in depicting with force, clarity, delicacy, and harmony. Poetry is harmonious eloquence. M. Pascal must have had very little taste to be able to say that *fatal laurel, fair luminary,* and other such nonsense are poetical beauties; and the editors of these *Pensées* must have been persons very little versed in literature to have printed a reflection so unworthy of its illustrious author.

I do not send you my other remarks on the *Pensées* of M. Pascal; they would drag out the discussion too long. It is enough to have thought to find certain errors of inattention in this great genius. It is consoling to so limited an intelligence as mine to be convinced that the greatest men can be wrong like the common herd.

APPENDIX

It is particularly interesting to know what the author of *Candide* (1759) thought of Pope's *Essay on Man* (1733-34), which came out too late to be mentioned in the *Philosophical Letters* as originally written. With an admiration of Pope which, however qualified, he never forswears, he writes on February 12, 1736, to Pierre Joseph Thoulier d'Olivet:

> Have you a translation of Pope's *Essay on Man?* It is a beautiful poem in English—though with ideas running through it that are quite false—on happiness.[1]

For the 1756 edition of his works, Voltaire changed the end of Letter XXII, after "Mollesse in *le Lutrin*," to read as follows.

The *Essay on Man* of Pope seems to me the most beautiful, most useful, most sublime didactic poem ever written in any language. It is true that the whole groundwork of it is to be found in Lord Shaftesbury's *Characteristics*, and I do not know why Mr. Pope gives the honor solely to Lord Bolingbroke, without saying a word about Shaftesbury, the pupil of Locke.

Everything related to metaphysics has been thought in all periods and among all peoples who cultivate the mind, and this system much resembles that of Leibniz, which maintains that, of all possible worlds, God must have chosen the best, and that in this best it was necessary that the irregularities of our globe and the stupidities of its inhabitants should have their place. It also resembles that idea of Plato's that in the infinite chain of beings, our earth, our body, our soul are among the necessary links. But neither Leibniz nor Pope allows of the changes that Plato imagines to have happened to these links, to our souls and our bodies. Plato spoke as a poet in his not very intelligible prose, and Pope speaks as a philosopher in his admirable verses. He says that

[1] Number 978 of Besterman's edition of the letters.

everything has been from the beginning as it has had to be, and as it is.

I have been flattered, I confess, to see that he agrees with me in something I said some years ago: "You are surprised that God should have made man so limited, so ignorant, so unhappy. Why are you not surprised that he didn't make him more limited, more ignorant, and more unhappy?" [2] When a Frenchman and an Englishman think the same, they must certainly be right.

The son of the famous Racine has printed a letter from Pope, addressed to him, in which Pope recants. That letter is written in the tone and style of M. de Fénelon. It was brought to him, he says, by Ramsay,[3] the editor of Télémaque; Ramsay the imitator of Télémaque, as Boyer [4] was of Corneille; Ramsay the Scot, who wanted to belong to the Académie Française; Ramsay, who regretted not being a doctor of the Sorbonne. But one thing I know, along with all the men of letters in England, is that Pope, with whom I have spent much time, could hardly read French; that he didn't speak a word of our language; that he never wrote a letter in French; that he was incapable of it; and that, if he did write this letter to the son of our Racine, it must have been that toward the end of his life God suddenly gave him the gift of tongues, as recompense for so admirable a work as his *Essay on Man*.[5]

Pope, he says in the "Poem on Natural Law" (c. 1751; pub. 1756), "carried the torch into the abyss of being, and man with his aid alone began to know himself." In the preface to his poem (published at the same time) on the Lisbon Disaster, the earthquake that on the first of November, 1755, had caused the death of some thirty thousand persons, Voltaire

2 See section XXVIII, Letter XXV.

3 Andrew Michael Ramsay (1686-1743), "the Chevalier de Ramsay," knight of the order of St. Lazarus. His imitation of his friend Fénelon's *Télémaque* is *Les Voyages de Cyrus, avec un Discours sur la Mythologie des Payens* (Paris, 1727). It was translated into English and reprinted with additions for nearly a century.

4 Abbé Claude Boyer (1618-98), author of many plays and member of the academy.

5 The original MS of the letter, written in English, was found in our own time, by Professor Émile Audra, in the Bibliothèque Nationale.

assures us that the theological objections made against the *Essay on Man* have not harmed it in the least; then he says,

> The author of the poem on the "Lisbon Disaster" does not combat the illustrious Pope, whom he has always admired and loved: he thinks like him on almost all points; but, profoundly conscious of the woes of mankind, he rises up against the abuse that is currently made of the ancient axiom *All is well.* He adopts that sad and more ancient truth, recognized by all men, that *there is evil on the earth;* he avows that the phrase *All is well,* taken in an absolute sense and without hope of a future, is nothing but an insult to the sorrows of our life.

When you announce that "All is well," he tells us in this poem on the earthquake, the universe gives you the lie, and your heart refutes your mind a hundred times over. All things are at war, and the innocent, as well as the guilty, undergo inevitable evil in this universe of eternal disorder. God is either a father indiscriminately punishing his children, all of whom are born guilty of original sin, or else he is a serenely indifferent First Cause. The truth of the matter can come to us only through revelation—and certainty about revelation is a cause of persecution and war. Though his poem is alive with pity and indignation at the condition of man, Voltaire says at the end that he does not rise up against Providence: he knows how to suffer but not how to complain. He also knows he had better be careful what he says.

He is still full of the subject in a letter written to Elie Bertrand on February 18, 1756:

> Evil is on the earth, and I should be mocking myself to say that a thousand unhappy people make for happiness. Yes, there is evil, and few men would care to begin their careers over again, perhaps not one in a hundred thousand. And when I am told that it all couldn't be otherwise, reason is outraged and so are my own afflictions. A workman with bad materials and bad instruments can quite understandably explain that he "couldn't do it any other way." But my poor Pope, my poor hunchback, whom I have known, whom

I have loved—who told you that God could not have made you without a hump? You smile at the apple story. Yet humanly speaking, and putting the sacred aside, it is more reasonable than the optimism of Leibniz: it explains why you are a hunchback, ill, and a little malicious.

We need a god who speaks to the human race. Optimism leads to despair. It is a cruel philosophy under a consoling name. Alas! if all is well when all is in pain, we shall be able to go on to a thousand worlds, where we shall suffer, and where all will be well. We shall go from misfortune to misfortune, looking for a better state. And if *all is well,* how do the Leibnizians make room for something better? This *better*—isn't it a proof that all is not well? And then—who doesn't know that Leibniz had no expectation of anything better. Just between us, my dear sir, all of them—Leibniz and Shaftesbury and Bolingbroke and Pope—were only trying to be clever. As for me, I suffer and I say so.[6]

On November 4, 1758, he writes in English to George Keith, the tenth Earl Marischal,

This present war is the most hellish that was ever fought. Y^r lordship saw formerly one battle a year at the most. But nowadays the earth is cover'd with blood and mangled carcasses, almost every month. Let the happy madmen who say that all what is, is well, be confounded. T'is not so indeed with twenty provinces exhausted and with three hundred thousand men murdered.[7]

Then comes *Candide,* and after it his long fever of rage against philosophical optimism subsides, for as Charles Philip Theodore of Sulzbach, the Elector Palatine, remarks to Voltaire on February 23, 1759,

Optimism has long since been banished from our globe, and if Pope were still living I doubt that he would maintain, seeing all that has happened in the last few years, that "all what is, is right." [8]

6 Besterman 6066.

7 Besterman 7220.

8 Besterman 7422. The quotation marks are mine: these words are in English.